Creative
Paper Quilts

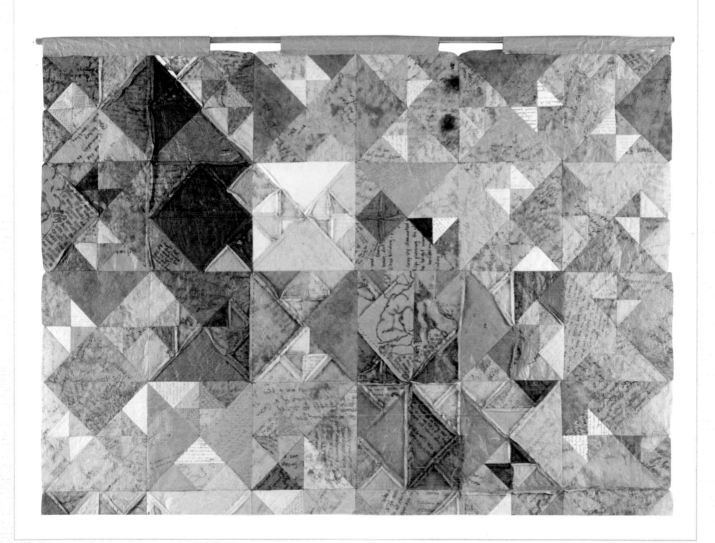

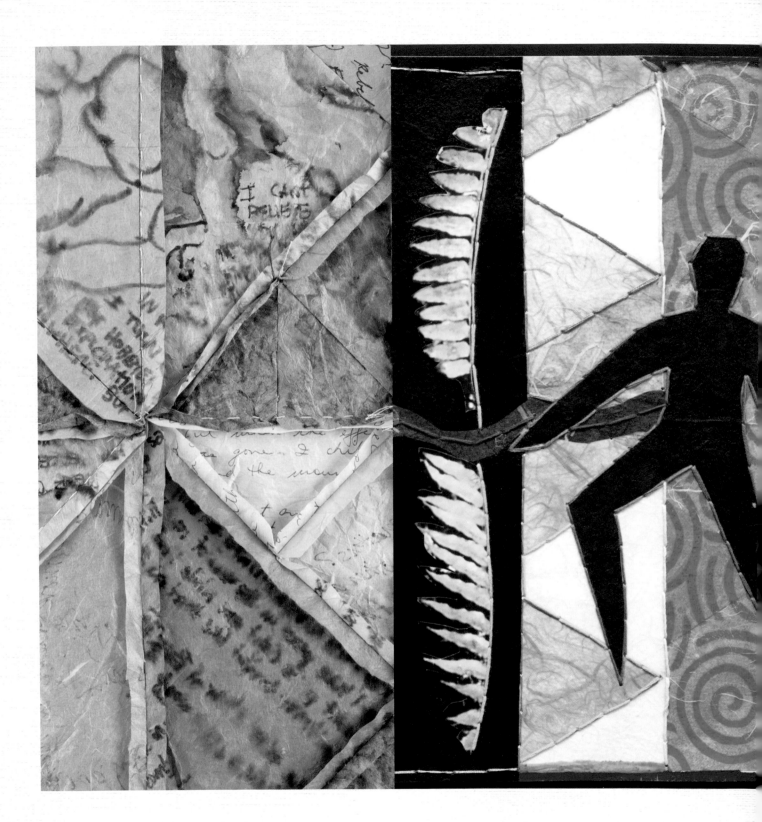

Creative
Paper Quilts

Appliqué, Embellishment,
Patchwork, Piecework

Terri Stegmiller

LARK BOOKS

A Division of Sterling Publishing Co., Inc.
New York / London

A Red Lips 4 Courage Communications, Inc., book

www.redlips4courage.com

Eileen Cannon Paulin
President
Catherine Risling
Director of Editorial

Editor: Lecia Monsen
Copy Editors: Catherine Risling, Ashlea Scaglione
Art Director: Jocelyn Foye
Illustrations: Jerry Ford
Photographer: Gregory Case

Library of Congress Cataloging-in-Publication Data

Stegmiller, Terri.
Creative paper quilts : appliqué, embellishment, patchwork, piecework /
Terri Stegmiller. -- 1st ed.
    p. cm.
ISBN-13: 978-1-60059-312-3 (hc-plc with jacket : alk. paper)
ISBN-10: 1-60059-312-7 (hc-plc with jacket : alk. paper)
1. Quilting--Patterns. 2. Paper work. I. Title.
TT835.S7145 2008
746.46'041--dc22
                                    2008004156
10 9 8 7 6 5 4 3 2 1

First Edition

Published by Lark Books,
A Division of Sterling Publishing Co., Inc.
387 Park Avenue South, New York, NY 10016

Text © 2008, Terri Stegmiller
Photography © 2008, Red Lips 4 Courage Communications, Inc.
Illustrations © 2008, Red Lips 4 Courage Communications, Inc.

Distributed in Canada by Sterling Publishing, c/o Canadian Manda Group,
165 Dufferin Street
Toronto, Ontario, Canada M6K 3H6

Distributed in the United Kingdom by GMC Distribution Services,
Castle Place, 166 High Street, Lewes, East Sussex, England BN7 1XU

Distributed in Australia by Capricorn Link (Australia) Pty Ltd.,
P.O. Box 704, Windsor, NSW 2756 Australia

If you have questions or comments about this book, please contact:
Lark Books
67 Broadway
Asheville, NC 28801
(828) 253-0467

Manufactured in China

ISBN 13: 978-1-60059-312-3

For information about custom editions, special sales, premium and corporate
purchases, please contact Sterling Special Sales Department at (800) 805-5489 or
specialsales@sterlingpub.com.

Table of Contents

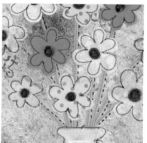

"*The very first paper quilt I made was hard. I was used to work-ing with fabric, not paper. At first the process was awkward and difficult and I figured that I'd try it once and that'd be it. Once I was done I couldn't figure out why I was being so stubborn about it. I loved my results! Each paper quilt since has been a joy to make and I'm thrilled that the paper-quilting phenomenon is occurring during my artistic lifetime.*"

—Terri Stegmiller, *author*

Introduction

Welcome to the growing world of paper quilts. I invite you to join me in this fabulous way to create quilts and quilted projects. I enjoy many crafts, especially making wall hangings and art pieces. Once I learned how to make quilts from paper, I felt a whole new world had opened with unlimited possibilities.

Paper is an ever-present part of modern life. Just consider how many times a day you use some sort of paper product—too many times to count I'm sure. I would equate the wide variety of available paper types to being like a child in a candy store. From beautiful handmade papers to everyday bits and pieces that would normally be tossed in the trash, the sources for art are endless.

When I think of a quilt, my mind conjures up an image of a cozy blanket to snuggle under on a cold, stormy day. That's what quilts were traditionally designed and used for, so the idea of combining them may seem extraordinary. Quilts have evolved over time to become more than just a blanket. Today, we have quilts that are created as works of art, and some are made using very nontraditional materials. The paper quilts in this book are beautiful interpretations of fabric quilts using techniques such as traditional piecing, appliqué, and more.

Making the transition from working with fabrics to working with paper is really not difficult. In fact, you'll soon find that looking for the perfect paper is just as much fun as the hunt for the ideal fabric. If you are already working with papers, you've got it made. You probably have most of the tools and materials to create a unique paper quilt already.

Flipping through the pages of this book, you'll see how the artists created these amazing quilts and will be encouraged to make your own. From choosing a design, to learning about materials and techniques, to putting it all together to make your own paper quilt—you will quickly become immersed in the enjoyable world of paper quilting. Whether you prefer quilts of a traditional style or are inclined to be more inventive, I'm confident there is a wide variety of projects you'll enjoy making.

Terri Stegmiller

Chapter 1
Getting Started

As with any art project, there are some tools and materials you will need in order to create paper quilts. If you already have a fabric or quilting background, or if you work in scrapbooking or other paper arts, then you probably already have many of the tools needed. If you are like me, you will be eager to add a new tool or product to your studio. Using the right tools for the job on hand is as necessary as having the correct ingredients when baking. The right tool or material will help you achieve a more professional look when your piece is completed.

Some of the projects in this book are created using the specific techniques taught in this chapter. Some of these methods may be familiar to you, but some may be new. You will find that once you learn these skills, you will be able to use them on other types of art projects too.

The artists who have contributed projects to this book each have developed their own unique way of doing things. You, too, will find that some techniques work well for you, while others do not. Explore and investigate new approaches and don't be afraid to tailor them to your way of working. It's always fun when you discover a tool or technique that helps make your artwork easy and beautiful.

Materials
Tools
Techniques

Materials

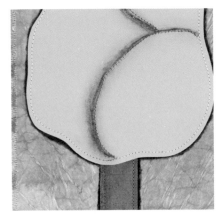

Adhesives

Most paper adhesives fall into two groups: permanent and temporary. Permanent adhesives bond quickly and items cannot be removed once the glue begins to dry. They are available in many different formats, the most common being white craft glue, also known as polyvinyl acetate (PVA); glue sticks; tape runner dispensers; glue dots; double-sided tape; adhesive sprays; acrylic gel medium; decoupage medium; and fusible web.

Temporary adhesives allow elements to be repositioned while you are working. These are also available in many of the same formats as permanent adhesives. Make sure the packaging says it is temporary or repositionable.

Drafting tape is an excellent tool for holding paper quilts together temporarily. It was originally designed for architects and engineers to hold drawings on their drawing boards while they worked and was easily removed when the drawing was done. It doesn't leave any residue on the paper and is also acid-free.

Batting

The unseen middle layer of a quilt is traditionally created with batting. Batting is made from many different fibers such as cotton, polyester, silk, or wool, and adds dimension and support to a quilt as well as warmth. Since paper quilts aren't made for warmth, the batting layer can be anything you choose, as long as you can stitch through it. I find that traditional fabric quilt battings are a bit too soft for working with paper, so I use a heavyweight interfacing instead. This type of interfacing provides a rigid, supportive base for paper quilt projects.

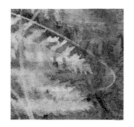

Brushes

You will need paintbrushes to add color to your papers. When I add background color to a project, I usually use an inexpensive paintbrush, available at most hardware stores in sizes that range from half an inch and up. I use artist brushes if I'm going to be painting a focal design such as a face. I keep an assortment of sizes and bristle types on hand so that I can easily choose the brush that best fits my needs.

Charcoal Pencils

I like to add depth and shading to my art and have found charcoal pencils to be an excellent tool for this task. They are available in a variety of hardness grades. It's a good idea to experiment with different grades to choose the one that works best for you. An alternative to charcoal pencils is black acrylic paint thinned with water to the desired consistency.

Charcoal pencils come in a variety of grades. The softer charcoal creates wide, dark lines and is excellent for shading, while the harder grade is good for adding defined lines and accents.

Color

There are many ways and reasons to add color to your paper project, and there are many products on the market that will work. One product I like to use when I create fabric-backed paper is a paint-like dye. These dyes are ready to use right out of the bottle with no powders or chemicals to mix. These work best on fabrics but they can also be used with paper, especially with absorbent papers such as tissue paper.

Acrylic paints, color wash sprays, sprayable watercolors, and inkpads are also useful for adding additional color to your projects. Gesso is yet another product I like to use. When it's applied sparingly, gesso adds a whitewashed look to paper. It's a good idea to have a palette when working with acrylic paints, or you can use a paper plate to hold puddles and mix colors.

Fabric

I do use some fabric when paper quilting. I use 100-percent cotton muslin for the backing layer and hanging sleeve if I will be hanging a quilt project directly on the wall. Since I'm working in paper, there's no need to prewash the fabrics.

Another method I used to incorporate fabric is when I make fabric-backed paper. I often use fabric-backed paper as a background on paper quilts. It is a stable, supportive surface and I love the textures and colors that result. I typically use muslin, but other fabrics that work well are 100-percent cotton, cotton-polyester blends, or lightweight cotton duck or canvas. White or off-white fabrics work best if I plan to add color to the fabric-backed paper.

Paper

There are many types of papers to choose from when creating paper quilts. Listed here are a few: scrapbook, handmade, art papers, tissue, gift wrap, paper towels, book pages, newspapers, calendars, napkins, notepads (with or without writing), magazines, junk mail, envelopes, vellum, ephemera, silk, stickers, cardboard or chipboard, paper bags, cardstock, postcards, old sewing pattern tissue. This list could go on and on because the sky's the limit when it comes to paper sources. Besides the different types of papers listed, there are also variations within those types such as thickness, printed design, texture, and color.

Once you start saving paper, you'll find that adding to your stash becomes second nature. Opening the day's mail will have you noticing the inside designs printed on envelopes. When going to the movies, you'll be less hesitant to toss the ticket stub, and paging through magazines will have a whole new meaning.

There are stores that specialize in selling all types of paper products for crafting, writing, and more. Many art, craft, and scrapbook stores sell a variety of papers that are perfect for paper quilts. If you don't have a store nearby, there is also the Internet. You will find an endless supply of papers such as handmade, art, and more. Simply search for art, decorative, or handmade paper and you'll be flooded with options.

Pens and Markers

When you want to add fine lines, details, or writing to a paper quilt, consider using permanent markers, gel pens, or colored pencils. All are available in a wide variety of colors and tip sizes as well as permanent or water-soluble and archival, which is generally lightfast.

Spray Fixative

Charcoal, chalk, and other products that smear easily can be controlled with a spray fixative product. Fixatives are found in the art section of a craft store, near the drawing and sketching supplies. Always use these products according to the manufacturer's directions and in a well-ventilated area.

Stamps

Stamped designs on papers can provide an additional level of artistic flair to your project. Stamps are available in a wide range of forms such as rubber stamps, which come either mounted on a wood block or unmounted, foam, and hand-carved. Hand-carved stamps are created on linoleum blocks specifically designed for hand carving or soft vinyl blocks. Special tools are available to carve the blocks to create your own design for stamping. Stamps can be used with acrylic paints, inkpads, or markers. Be sure to thoroughly clean the stamps between each color application. You can use a specially made stamp cleaner fluid or simple window cleaner sprayed on a double thickness of paper towel.

Rubber stamps add a unique touch to paper quilts. Use stamp sets for a more cohesive look or mix and match styles for a customized flair.

Tools

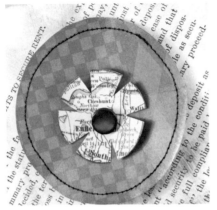

Awl

An awl is a handheld tool with a sharp, tapered point used for punching holes in fabric and paper (see Fig. 1). This aids in attaching embellishments to your project. A hole punch is a good alternative as long as the hole you are making is close to the edge of your work.

Fig. 1

Cutting Implements

When it comes to cutting your paper into the sizes and shapes you need for your project, there are a few ways you can do this.

Scissors are one of the most simple tools. Along with the basic pair, you will find that there are a number of specialty scissors available that will produce a decorative design as you cut. Remember, if you also work with fabric, you should keep a pair of scissors designated just for paper and a pair just for fabric. Paper cutting will dull the scissors' blades quickly and you don't want to ruin a good pair of fabric scissors.

Rotary cutting tools work well for cutting paper. Again, you will want to invest in a second rotary cutter or keep extra blades on hand for using with paper. Rotary cutting tools include a cutting mat; a hand-held rotary cutting tool that holds a round, very sharp blade; and a see-through ruler.

Foam Stamps

Foam stamps are similar to rubber stamps. These are typically used with fabric stamping but you can also use them with paper. I like these types of stamps because they have bold, less intricate designs than rubber stamps.

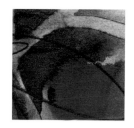

Hand Sewing

If you choose to hand sew your paper quilt, be sure to have a variety of embroidery needle sizes on hand to accommodate different thicknesses of paper and thread types. There is an abundance of threads and fibers available and if any of them are too thick for stitching through your paper quilt, they can always be couched down. *Note: Couching is explained in the Techniques section.* The most commonly used threads for hand stitching are embroidery floss, perle cottons, and even machine threads.

You should use a thimble when hand sewing to protect your finger. Pushing the needle through layers of paper can be a bit more difficult than pushing a needle through fabric.

Rubber Stamps

These stamps are available in mounted and unmounted forms. I've used both and personally prefer the mounted type because they give me something to hold onto. There are temporary mounts available for unmounted stamps.

Sewing Machine

A sewing machine is a helpful tool when making paper quilts, but it's not a "must-have." It is possible to sew paper by hand, although it is a little more difficult than sewing fabric because of the thickness of some papers. There are simple, inexpensive sewing machines available in the scrapbook arena as well as full-blown sewing machines used to sew clothing and other involved fabric projects. Choose what works best for your skills and budget.

Your sewing machine need not have a lot of bells and whistles. As long as it can do basic straight and zigzag stitches, it will work fine for paper sewing. Machines that have the capability of either lowering the feed dogs or covering them with a special throat plate can be used for free-motion stitching.

Template Plastic

Template plastic is available in several different thicknesses, usually clear or with pre-marked grids. I like to use a thin, clear plastic so that the view of the pattern underneath is not obstructed. You will use template plastic to trace the project pattern pieces found in Chapter 7.

 Try This

The feed dogs on a sewing machine are located beneath the presser foot and look somewhat like teeth. They help move the fabric under the presser foot. Most machines have a switch to lower the feed dogs so they won't grab the fabric to move it.

Techniques

Designing a Paper Quilt

Designing a paper quilt is much like designing a fabric quilt, whether you prefer traditional, appliqué, collage, or artistic style. Choose the design, decide on the dimensions, and proceed from there. Most quilt blocks intended for fabric work well with paper quilting. As you plan, keep in mind that paper isn't as flexible as fabric. If the quilt gets too big and you need to sew on an area in the middle of the piece, it will be difficult to manipulate the project under the arm of the sewing machine. However, if you plan accordingly you should be able to easily add rows of blocks to your quilt. If you wish to add some stitched details to the surface once the quilt is constructed, you may need to add those details with hand stitching.

Ideas for quilts can be found in many places and the most obvious is patterns intended for fabric quilts. Another great source is coloring books; or, if you like to create unique designs, simply draw your own pattern. This is the method I typically use to create my quilts. I normally begin a design with sketches in my sketchbook, and then I cut a piece of paper to the size of my finished quilt and draw the design to size. I do the preliminary drawing in pencil so I can erase or make changes along the way. Once I have a final drawing in pencil, I go over the pencil lines with a permanent marker. This becomes the main pattern and I don't cut it apart. I leave it intact to act as a map and reference. I will sometimes make notes on this main pattern to help in the design process.

The next step is to make templates for the major elements in the design. Lay a piece of clear template plastic over each design element and trace. Mark the right side of the template. *Note: When you lay these template pieces on the backside of the paper, remember to place them right side down, otherwise you will get a design that is the reverse of your main pattern.*

Once your templates are cut out, simply place them on your chosen papers and trace around them. Cut out the paper pieces and place them on the background paper.

Sometimes I design paper quilts as I go. For example, a collage-style quilt isn't one I typically plan in advance. I just start laying out papers and arranging and rearranging them until I get a look that excites me. Working in this method is very liberating and can lead to exciting new discoveries.

Bonding

There isn't one ideal way to bond two layers of paper together—it's more or less a matter of preference. For large pieces of paper, I prefer to use fusible web, which is basically very fine sheets of glue. It is available with or without a paper backing. I follow the instructions on the package for applying the web to the paper surface. Once the fusible web is adhered to the paper, cut out the shape and then lay it with the fusible side down on the background surface. Apply heat with an iron, following the package directions. I use a sheet of baking parchment to protect both the ironing surface and the iron from any stray fusible web.

When using other types of glue, I test it on the paper I plan to use. Some papers, such as very thin or absorbent papers, may discolor or change appearance when the glue is applied. This typically happens with liquid glues. I don't find this to be as much of a problem with glue sticks or other types of solid glues, but I still perform the test to be sure.

I generally use three different types of glues when making paper quilts: a glue stick, glue pen, and a tape runner. I use the tape runner with paper pieces that are as wide or wider than the dispenser. I like this glue because it is easy to use, less messy, and won't soak through the paper. When working with small shapes, I use either a glue stick or glue pen. The glue pen resembles a marker and is a liquid form of glue that is easy to apply on thin pieces of paper. Use the gluing/bonding method that works best for you, but take the time to test your glues on the paper you choose.

Stitching on Paper

Stitching a paper quilt with a sewing machine is much the same as stitching fabric. There are two main things to keep in mind. First, you will need to plan the stitching carefully. If you stitch in an area that you didn't want stitching, the needle holes will show when you remove the thread. Second, use a stitch length that isn't too small or too close. If you stitch with very small stitches, the holes will create a perforated line and the paper may lift or fall apart. I suggest using a normal stitch length, which is a setting that is approximately 2.4 mm when stitching a straight stitch.

I use two basic machine stitches when stitching my paper quilts. The straight stitch (see Fig. 1) is the most basic stitch of all sewing machines.

‒‒‒‒‒‒‒‒‒‒‒‒‒‒‒‒‒‒‒‒‒‒‒‒

Fig. 1

The other stitch I use often is the zigzag stitch (see Fig. 2). I use this stitch setting when I want to add some extra excitement to my project; the jaggedness of this stitch is perfect for this effect. The zigzag stitch and the satin stitch are very similar. A satin stitch is basically a zigzag stitch with a very short stitch length. The satin-stitched threads will be close together and you won't be able to see the fabric or paper beneath the stitch.

∧∧∧∧∧∧∧∧∧∧∧∧∧∧∧∧∧∧∧∧

Fig. 2

Another type of machine stitching I use is known as free-motion stitching (see Fig. 3). With this method, the machine's feed dogs are lowered or covered, depending on the sewing machine, and the stitch length is set to zero. You have full control over the movement and the direction of the stitches because the feed dogs are not controlling the movement of the material. With this method you can move the material any way you choose. It's very much like drawing, except that you are moving the paper instead of the drawing tool.

A special foot, typically a darning foot, is needed with free-motion stitching. They are available in metal and clear plastic.

Try free-motion stitching by starting with a fabric sample. A 12" (30.5 cm) square is a good size to use for practice. Baste, fuse, or adhere a piece of fabric with temporary adhesive to both sides of a piece of batting. Use a thread color that will show well so you can see what you are doing. Begin stitching with a couple of tiny stitches to secure the thread. Start moving the fabric in circular movements while going fairly fast with the needle movement. Doodle and draw until the entire piece is covered. Remember that the speed of the needle is always faster than the movement with your hands. As with most techniques, free-motion stitching does take some practice, but it is a fun technique to learn.

Hand Stitching

Another way to add some extra pizzazz to your paper quilt is by incorporating some hand stitches. This will allow you to use threads and fibers that would be difficult to stitch by machine. If you find that stitching through the paper layers is too difficult, pre-punch some holes where you want

Fig. 3

your needle to go using the tip of a stitching awl or a quilter's T-pin. Remember to plan carefully where you want your stitching holes, because once they are punched, you can't change them without starting the entire project over.

Because paper quilts aren't as flexible as fabric, some hand embroidery stitches may be difficult to execute. Here are a few basic hand stitches that are easier to work with on paper.

Couching

This is a technique in which yarn or other material is laid across the surface and fastened in place with small stitches of the same or different yarn or thread (see Fig. 4). Lay the yarn where you want it to be stitched. Thread an embroidery needle with another thread and knot the end. Come up at point A right next to the yarn laid on the surface. Push the needle down at point B on the other side of the yarn on the surface. Continue this pattern of stitching across the length of the surface yarn. You can space the stitches as close together or as far apart as you wish.

Fig. 4

Running stitch

This is a basic stitch in hand sewing. It is worked by passing the needle in and out of the fabric following a marked or imaginary line (see Fig. 5). Running stitches may be of varying

length, but typically more thread is visible on the top of the sewing than on the underside.

French knot

The French knot resembles a small ball or knot on the stitching surface. It can be made smaller by a single wrap of thread around the needle or larger by adding more wraps around the needle. Typically a French knot is made by wrapping thread two or three times around the needle and then inserting the needle back in the surface next to where it emerged (see Fig. 6). Hold the thread taut once the needle is wrapped and while inserting the needle back into the surface to create a nice, tight knot.

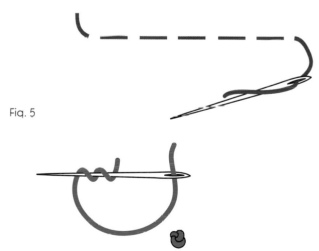

Fig. 5

Fig. 6

Making Fabric-Backed Paper

To make fabric-backed paper you will need white cotton muslin or fabric of your choice,

tissue paper, a mixing bowl, water, polyvinyl acetate (PVA) glue, and a paintbrush. I use white fabric and basic white gift-wrap tissue paper because I like to color my fabric-backed paper in the color scheme of my choosing. Cut the fabric the same size as the tissue paper and lay it out flat on a protected work surface.

Prepare the water and glue mixture by mixing equal amounts of water and glue in the mixing bowl. Brush glue mixture over the fabric, ensuring that all areas are wet. *Note: If you have leftover glue mixture, store it in an airtight container for next time. Just be sure to mix it well before the next use, as the glue will have settled.*

Scrunch the piece of tissue paper into a ball, making sure there are a lot of wrinkles to add texture to the end result. Carefully spread the tissue paper out on the workspace surface, away from the wet fabric, and smooth it to flatten.

Lay the tissue on top of the wet fabric and press down, carefully smoothing the tissue to remove air bubbles as you go. Some bubbles may be difficult to remove; I suggest leaving them or you may tear a hole in the tissue.

Spread another coat of the glue mixture on the tissue, ensuring that the entire piece is covered. Wrinkles will form in the tissue paper but these will provide texture in the finished paper.

Adding color to fabric-backed paper
Apply color to the tissue while the glue mixture is still wet. Using either a watered-down acrylic paint or dye-type paint, squirt or brush two or three colors onto the tissue. The wetness of the tissue paper helps the color spread and blend.

Use a clean, damp brush to gently blend the colors together and cover all the areas of the tissue paper with color. Brush in one direction or go over it in several directions if you prefer the colors to blend more.

Let the fabric-backed paper dry flat up to 24 hours, depending on the climate conditions. When the paper is dry, carefully peel it away from the plastic sheeting. The paper tends to curl so flatten it with an iron. Use a sheet of parchment to protect the iron and ironing surface.

Painting on Paper
There may be times when you have a piece of paper you want to use in your project, but you'd like to change the color. This can be done by painting the paper with acrylic or watercolor paints. Both types of paint are readily accessible, inexpensive, and easy to clean up, and come in a range of colors that can be mixed to create new colors.

Watercolor paints are more transparent and are ideal if the paper has a preprinted design because the design will show through the paint. Mixing in more water with a watercolor paint creates a lighter shade. The best way to apply watercolor paint to paper is with an artist's paintbrush, but it can be sprayed on as well.

Acrylic paints are available in transparent and opaque forms and even metallic colors. You can create a wash with acrylic paints by adding water to them—the more water, the thinner the coverage. Acrylic paint can be applied with paintbrushes, foam brushes, stamps, and stencils.

Stamping
Stamping images on paper is easy and fun and there are many designs to choose from to accent your project.

I use either acrylic paints or inkpads with stamps. To use paints, squirt some onto a palette. Use a small sponge to dip into the paint and then dab the excess onto the palette. Dab the sponge onto the stamp until it's completely covered and then press the stamp firmly onto the paper surface. Reload the stamp with more paint and repeat. To use the inkpad, simply press the stamp onto the pad's surface and then onto the paper. You can either reload the paint or ink between each application or stamp several times without refreshing the color for a gradually softened image.

Adding Embellishments

Embellishing your project is like putting the sprinkles on the frosting of a cake. Embellishments add sparkle and dimension, and draw the viewer closer. Use beads, buttons, sequins, drawings, ribbons, fibers, and text. Secure accent pieces by sewing or gluing them onto the project. If you choose to glue them, be sure to use clear-drying, strong permanent glue.

Depending on the process used to create a paper quilt, you may need to wait to add embellishments until the end of the project; otherwise, they might get in the way of sewing or finishing the project.

Finishing the Edges

Once the paper quilt is completed, you'll need to finish the edges. There are different ways to do this. Choose one of the following methods, or develop a method of your own.

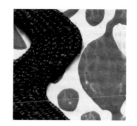

Traditional binding

Fabric quilts traditionally use a fabric binding, and this binding also works with paper quilts. Cut strips of fabric 1½" (3.81 cm) wide. With wrong sides together, fold in half lengthwise and press. Align the raw edge of one side of the folded strip to the raw edge of the paper quilt and sew using a straight stitch. Fold the fabric strip around the edge of the paper quilt to the backside. Hand-stitch the strip to the back.

This binding method can be done with one long strip that reaches around all four sides of your quilt. In this case, you would miter the fabric at the corners. On a mitered corner, the seam is sewn at a 45-degree angle to the edge of the quilt. If the fabric you are using isn't long enough to reach around all four sides, simply cut enough strips and sew them together at the ends to create one long strip. Another option is to apply four strips that are the same length as the sides of the quilt and attach each one separately.

Zigzag binding

A fast and easy method to finish the edge of a quilt is to zigzag stitch along all four sides. Set your machine to sew a wide zigzag stitch (a setting of 4 mm to 5 mm is ideal). If using a very short stitch length, the resulting look will resemble a satin stitch, where the stitching completely covers the edge. The setting on my machine that I prefer to use for zigzag stitching is between .6 and .9 mm. I use a smaller setting when sewing with a finer thread such as decorative rayon and a larger setting with a thicker thread such as quilting cotton.

Fused binding

Fuse either paper or fabric to the edges of a paper quilt. To do this, cut a strip of paper or fabric ½"–¾" (1.3–1.9 cm) wide. The length of the strip should match the length of the side of the quilt you are finishing. Apply fusible webbing to the backside of the paper or fabric strip. Lay the strip over the quilt, covering ¼" (.6 cm) of the edge and iron to fuse in place. Fold the remainder of the strip around to the backside and iron to fuse in place. Repeat with the remaining quilt edges.

Displaying a Quilt

Once your project is finished, you will probably want to display it. Here are a few ways to display a paper quilt.

Framed quilts

Framing your quilt under glass is a great choice if you want to protect it from getting soiled. You could also have it framed without using glass. Centering the quilt on a mat board in a coordinating color and inserting it into a frame is another good option for displaying your artwork.

Stretched canvas

Another great way to display your quilt is to attach it to stretched canvas. Stretched canvas is available at art and craft stores in many sizes, including custom sizes. You can choose to leave the canvas natural or paint it a coordinating color to set off the quilt. To attach the project to the canvas, simply use a clear monofilament thread or fishing line and stitch the four corners securely to the canvas. If the quilt is fairly large in size or particularly heavy, you may want to add some additional stitches along the sides, top, and bottom to secure it.

Add color accents to the canvas to set off the colors of the quilt that it will hold. The painting doesn't have to be perfect. The slight inconsistencies reinforce the handcrafted nature of the project.

The paper quilt project *Patty* is mounted on a stretched canvas that is painted in complementary colors selected from the project.

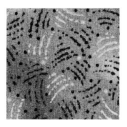

Hanging sleeve

A hanging sleeve is a fabric tube attached to the backside of the piece so that you can hang it on the wall. Typically a dowel, curtain rod, or decorative wrought iron rod can be inserted to

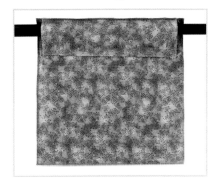

hold the quilt, as long as the sleeve is wide enough for the rod to fit through. I've even seen tree branches used to hang a quilt.

Creating a sleeve for a quilt is simple. The sleeve is attached to the quilt backing before it is attached to the quilt.

For this example, let's assume our finished project width is 12" (30.5 cm) square. Measure the quilt's finished width and cut a 12" x 7" (30.5 x 17.8 cm) piece of fabric. Determine how wide your hanging sleeve needs to be to hold the hanging rod. *Note: I tend to make my sleeves large enough to accommodate nearly any type of rod.* For this example I wanted a 3¼" (8.2 cm) wide sleeve. Multiply that measurement by two and add ½" (1.3 cm) for the seam allowance.

Fig. 7   Fig. 8

This gives you a cutting measurement of 7" (17.8 cm). Hem the two ends of the fabric by

folding ½" (1.3 cm) of one of the 7" (17.8 cm) ends, wrong sides together, and press with an iron (see Fig. 7). Fold over ½" (1.3 cm) again and press. Sew this seam to secure. The dashed line represents the sewn line (see Fig. 8). Repeat these steps on the opposite end.

Fold the fabric in half lengthwise, with right sides together. Sew a ¼" (.6 cm) seam to create a tube (see Fig. 9). Turn tube right side out and press with a warm iron.

Center the sleeve along one edge on the right side of the backing fabric. Topstitch the lower edge of the sleeve to the backing. The top edge of the sleeve will be secured when the edge of the quilt is finished (see Fig. 10).

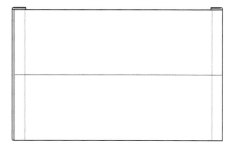

Fig. 9

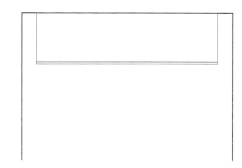

Fig. 10

Terri Stegmiller

Chapter 2

Appliqué Designs

The word appliqué comes from the French and simply means to secure one piece of material to another to create a design. This is a great technique for creating paper quilts that portray a scene or picture. It's so much fun to dream up quilts using the appliqué method and if you sketch on a regular basis, you may already have many ideas. Photographs, day-to-day family life, and the great outdoors can all inspire your next paper quilt.

Do you have a pet? Animals make excellent subjects for quilts. As you'll see in this chapter there are paper quilts that feature a cat or a dog. Nature is another inspiration for quilting. Flowers make wonderful subjects even when they aren't realistic. I sometimes prefer living in my own fantasy flower garden and enjoy creating fun, unique flowers. Dream up your own flower garden using one of the projects shown in this chapter.

Collage has become a very popular art form and is a fantastic idea for a paper quilt. Have fun experimenting with layers of paper and you will be excited when the arrangement speaks to you. Unleash your creative muse and you'll soon be provided with many ideas for unique paper quilts.

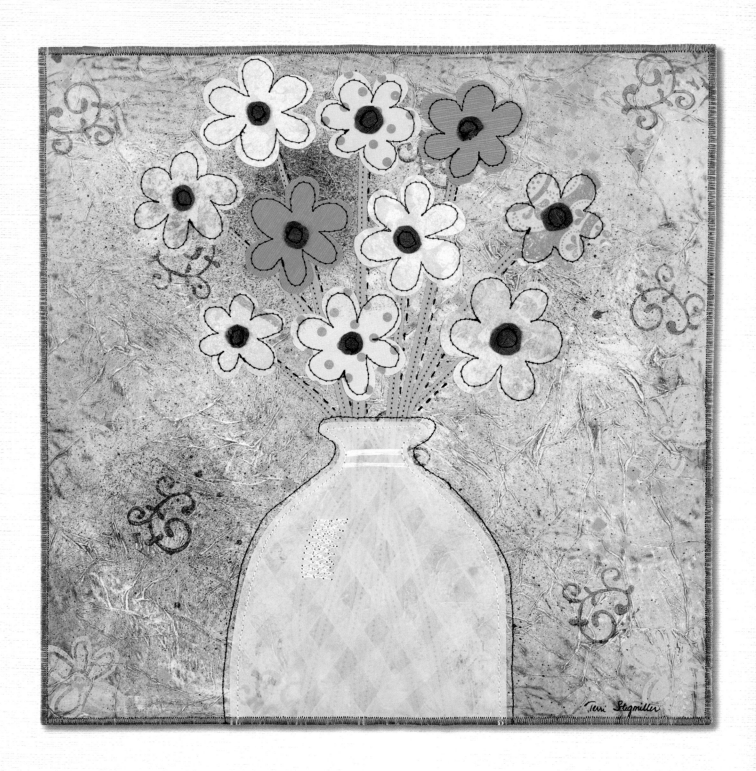

Vellum Vase

Terri Stegmiller
12" (30.5 cm) square

I love flowers. If I could have a vase of fresh flowers in my home every day, I would. Unfortunately this is not always possible because the nearest florist is some distance away. In order to satisfy my floral desires, I've created the illusion of an arrangement of fresh flowers with this quilt. The quilt makes me happy when I look at it and it is a good substitute for the real thing.

Materials

- Adhesive: temporary
- Fabric: 12" (30.5 cm) square
- Fabric-backed paper: 12" (30.5 cm) square
- Fine-point marker: black
- Fusible web: 12" (30.5 cm) square (2)
- Gel pen: white
- Heavyweight interfacing: 12" (30.5 cm) square
- Paper: 8½" x 11" (21.6 x 27.9 cm) assorted coordinating colors and patterns for flowers (3–4); green
- Pencil
- Thread: clear, coordinating colors (2–3)
- Vellum sheet: 8½" x 11" (21.6 x 27.9 cm)

Tools

- Iron and ironing surface
- Metal-edged ruler
- Scissors
- Sewing machine
- Template plastic

Instructions

Prepare the paper

1. Fuse the fabric-backed paper to the interfacing to create the background.

2. Trace the vellum Vase Patterns (page 120) onto the template plastic and cut them out. Place the flower template pieces on the backside of the desired papers and the vase on the vellum. Trace around the templates and cut them out. Cut freehand circles for the flower centers from coordinating colors of paper. These should vary in size and shape for a more natural look.

Make the arrangement

3. Cut long strips freehand from the green paper for the stems. Cut some straight and some with slight curves. Start cutting at about ¼" (.6 cm) wide for the stem bottoms and gradually narrow the cut as you proceed up the strip for the stem tops. *Note: It's best not to cut any pieces narrower than ⅛" (.3 cm) because it will be difficult to sew around them.*

4. Place the vase on the background in the desired position. Arrange the stems so they appear to be coming out of the vase yet they still reach the bottom of the vase. When you are satisfied with the arrangement, carefully remove the vase and glue the lower portions of the stems in place with temporary adhesive.

5. Add the flowers to the stems, overlapping them by ¼" (.6 cm) or more. Trim stems as necessary to achieve a pleasing arrangement. Once you are happy with the arrangement, secure everything with temporary adhesive.

6. Sew a straight stitch along the length of the stems using a coordinating color of thread. Carefully lift the flower at the top of the stem to continue stitching and then replace the flower. Lift the edges of any neighboring flowers if they overlap the stem you are stitching.

7. Place the vellum vase over the stems and align the bottom edge of the vase along the bottom edge of the background.

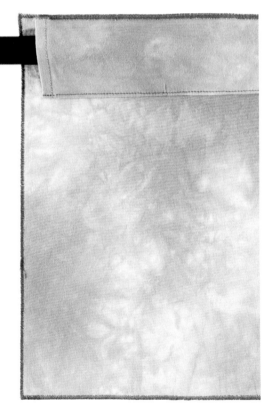

Color-coordinated fabric is used to back the quilt and create the hanging sleeve. The aqua color emphasizes the accent color on the front of the quilt.

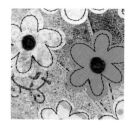
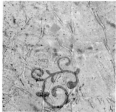

Secure the vase with temporary adhesive. Stitch around the vase ⅛" (.3 cm) from the edge using clear thread. Sew a wide zigzag stitch highlight on the vase. This highlight should have a slight curve to it.

8. Free-motion stitch around each flower ⅛" (.3 cm) from the edge using a coordinating thread color.

9. Glue a flower center to each flower and then free-motion stitch a circular shape inside each center.

10. Straight stitch an outline around the vase ⅛" (.3 cm) from the edge of the vellum on the background using a contrasting thread color.

Finish the quilt

11. Create a hanging sleeve, if desired, following the directions on page 23. Attach the sleeve to the fabric.

12. Fuse the fabric to the back of the interfacing, making certain the hanging sleeve is at the top of the quilt.

13. Zigzag stitch around the entire quilt, making sure to include the top edge of the hanging sleeve, if there is one. *Note: The recommended stitch width is 4–5 mm and the stitch length is .4–.8 mm but these may need to be adjusted, depending on the thickness of the thread used.*

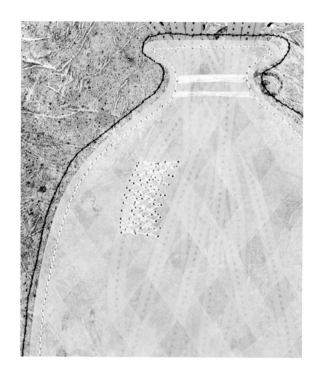

Try This

Draw designs such as random circles, spirals, or crosshatches to give the appearance of frosted glass on the vellum using a white gel pen. Add a line on the neck of the vase to suggest water. Draw a dashed line along the length of the stems that are above the vase with a black marker to highlight them.

Garden Breeze

Terri Stegmiller
12" (30.5 cm) square

I enjoy walking in the garden on a warm, sunny day, flowers swaying in the gentle breeze. That's the image I saw in my mind when I imagined this quilt. Summertime flowers come and go so quickly, but with this quilt hanging on the wall in the winter, I can always reminisce.

Materials

- Adhesive: temporary
- Fabric: 12" (30.5 cm) square
- Fabric-backed paper: 12" (30.5 cm) square
- Fusible web: 12" (30.5 cm) square (2)
- Heavyweight interfacing: 12" (30.5 cm) square
- Paper: 8½" x 11" (21.6 x 27.9 cm) assorted coordinating colors and patterns for flowers (3–4); green
- Pencil
- Thread: coordinating colors (3)

Tools

- Iron and ironing surface
- Metal-edged ruler
- Scissors
- Sewing machine
- Template plastic

Instructions

Prepare the paper

1. Fuse the fabric-backed paper to the interfacing to create the background.

2. Trace the Garden Breeze Patterns (page 120) onto the template plastic and cut them out. Place the template pieces on the backside of the desired papers. Trace around the templates and cut them out.

Make the arrangement

3. Cut long strips freehand from the green paper about ⅛" (.6 cm) wide for the flower stems.

4. Place the stems on the background at an angle and adhere with temporary adhesive.

5. Place a leaf on each stem and secure with temporary adhesive.

6. Add flower petals, overlapping the stems. Position some of the petals so they trail off the edge of the quilt. When you are pleased with the arrangement, secure with temporary adhesive. Trim excess petals that hang over the quilt edge.

7. Sew a straight stitch along both edges of each stem using a coordinating thread color. *Note: Lift up the flower petals to stitch under them as you go.*

8. Sew a straight stitch around the outer edge of each leaf and then stitch a center vein.

9. Zigzag stitch around each flower petal using a coordinating thread color.

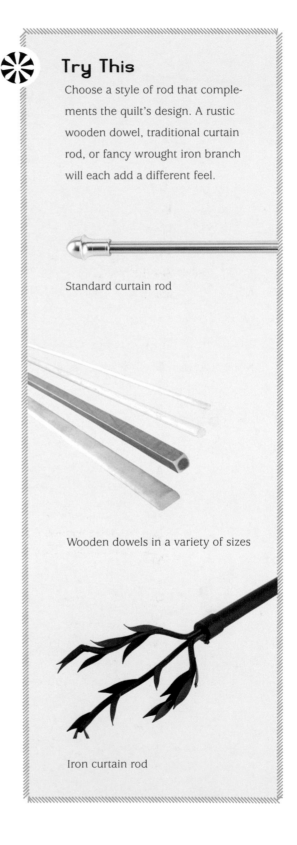

Try This

Choose a style of rod that complements the quilt's design. A rustic wooden dowel, traditional curtain rod, or fancy wrought iron branch will each add a different feel.

Standard curtain rod

Wooden dowels in a variety of sizes

Iron curtain rod

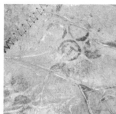

10. Place a flower center on each flower and adhere with temporary adhesive. Free-motion stitch a spiral in each center using a coordinating thread color.

Finish the quilt

11. Create a hanging sleeve, if desired, following the directions on page 23. Attach the sleeve to the fabric.

12. Fuse the fabric to the back of the interfacing, making certain the hanging sleeve is at the top of the quilt.

13. Zigzag stitch around the entire quilt, making sure to include the top edge of the hanging sleeve. *Note: The recommended stitch width is 4–5 mm and the stitch length is .4–.8 mm but these may need to be adjusted, depending on the thickness of the thread used.*

The mottled pattern and colors of the quilt back coordinate with the front without being an actual match.

✳ Try This

Use rubber stamps and coordinating inkpads to stamp designs on the fabric-backed paper background to give the illusion of flowers. You could also try using the eraser on a new pencil and acrylic paint to suggest flowers.

Patty

Terri Stegmiller
8" (20.3 cm) square

Many cats have touched my life and I find they always bring a smile to my face several times each day. One special cat, Patty, tugs at my heart. She's always eager to go on a walk with me and keep me company. She runs and plays and makes me laugh. I find myself drawing cats often in my sketchbook and this quilt came from one of those sketches.

Materials

- Acrylic paints: black, white
- Adhesives: permanent, temporary
- Fabric: 8" (20.3 cm) square
- Fabric-backed paper: 8" (20.3 cm) square
- Fusible web: 8" (20.3 cm) square (2)
- Heavyweight interfacing: 8" (20.3 cm) square
- Inkpad: white chalk
- Paper: 8½" x 11" (21.6 x 27.9 cm) coordinating color for background; coordinating colors and patterns for cat (3 – 4); white scrap
- Pencil
- Thread: coordinating colors (2)

Tools

- Iron and ironing surface
- Metal-edged ruler
- Paintbrush
- Scissors
- Sewing machine
- Template plastic

Instructions

Prepare the paper

1. Fuse the fabric-backed paper to the interfacing to create the background.

2. Trace the Patty Patterns (page 121) onto the template plastic and cut them out. Place the template pieces on the backside of the desired papers. Trace around the templates and cut them out.

3. Rub the inkpad randomly over the edges and surface of the paper pieces.

Make the cat

4. Position the paper pieces, except the nose and eyes, on the background and adhere with temporary adhesive.

5. Sew a straight stitch along all pieces about ⅛" (.3 cm) from the edges using a coordinating colored thread.

6. Sew straight stitch details on the cat's body, detailing the rounded back leg area, front legs, and chest using another coordinating colored thread. Refer to the project photo as needed.

7. Position nose and adhere with temporary adhesive.

8. Sew a straight stitch around the inside edges of nose.

9. Position eye whites and adhere with permanent adhesive.

10. Sew around the edge of each eye, not on the eye itself, and then extend the sewing line down to the nose as shown in the project photo.

11. Position iris on the whites and adhere with permanent adhesive.

12. Paint the pupils and whisker dots black. Add shading on each side of the nose, under the eyes, around the cheeks, and other areas as desired using a light brush of black paint.

13. Add highlights to the eyes and face with white paint as desired.

Finish the quilt

14. Create a hanging sleeve, if desired, following the directions on page 23. Attach the sleeve to the fabric.

15. Fuse the pieced fabric to the back of the interfacing, making certain the hanging sleeve is at the top of the quilt.

16. Zigzag stitch around the entire quilt, making sure to include the top edge of the hanging sleeve. *Note: The recommended stitch width is 4–5 mm and the stitch length is .4–.8 mm but these may need to be adjusted, depending on the thickness of the thread used.*

 Try This

Paint the irises of the eyes with acrylic paint instead of using paper for a more realistic look. Practice on a piece of scrap paper before painting on your project.

Boris

Variation of Patty

Terri Stegmiller

I know many people who are dog lovers. I prefer cats, but now and then I'll create a dog piece so the dog lovers I know will continue to like me. Am I bribing them? Probably, but I enjoy making dog art, too. Follow the same steps as the Patty project using the Boris Patterns on page 122 to create your own quilted canine companion.

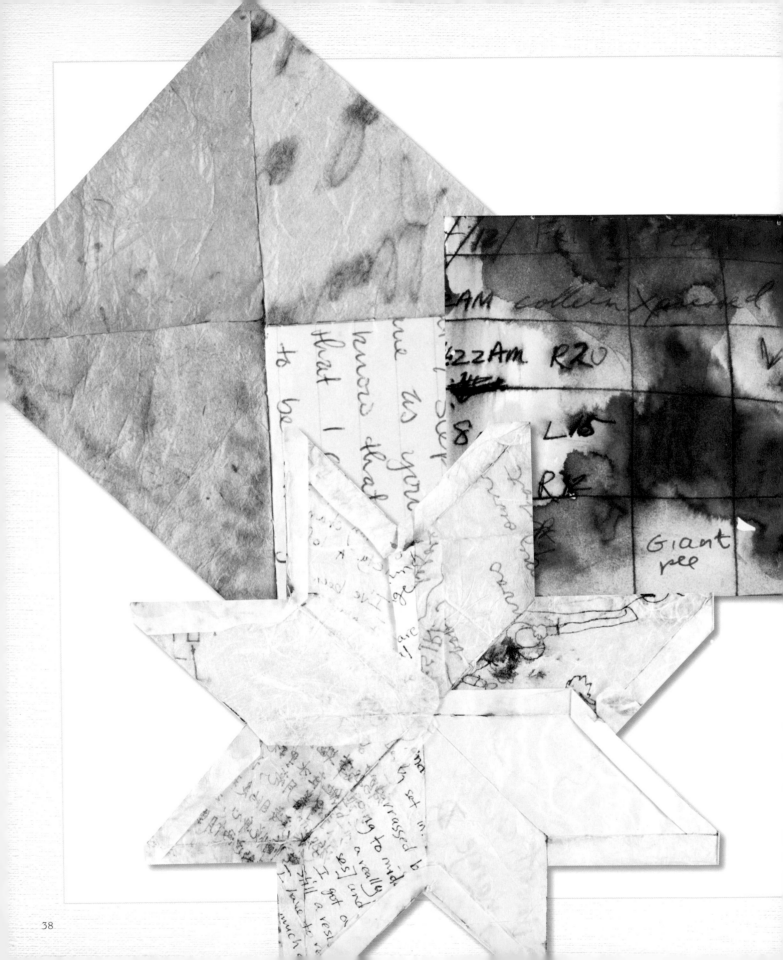

Chapter 3
Traditional Designs

Traditional quilting has roots far into the past. The passing of traditional beliefs and customs is a beautiful gift to each generation. Traditions give me a sense of family, security, and home. Most of us carry on some, if not all, of the traditions that were passed down to us; however, new generations may adapt or enhance the old or even create new traditions. For instance, making quilts with paper is definitely not traditional. Our ancestors certainly wouldn't have had a paper quilt on their bed to keep them warm.

Even though paper quilts aren't quite traditional, the projects you'll find in this chapter are patterned after traditional quilt blocks. The talented artist in this chapter shares her belief of the importance of family and incorporates love, wisdom, and memories in a truly wonderful piece of work. In another quilt she shares her many emotions of raising a child and captures a lasting memory.

There are hundreds of traditional quilt patterns that have been documented and I'm sure many more will be created as time goes by. Thinking of all of the possibilities for paper quilting, I smile at the idea of it becoming a time-honored tradition years from now.

Baby Quilt in Red
Family Quilt
Women's Wishing Quilt

Baby Quilt in Red

Colleen Kong-Savage

32" (81.2 cm) square

Motherhood was such a wallop to my senses. The idea that one tiny newborn brings on so much work performed on no sleep, an intensity of emotions, the number of people I suddenly depended on—all while recuperating from childbirth—was unfathomable. This project is an expression of the overwhelming experience of becoming a mother. I chose red for love, red-alert, blood, and vibrancy. Red is also the color of happiness in Chinese culture. For the "fabric" of the quilt I used my notes on breastfeeding times and poop observations, my husband's notes as he checked the babysitter's references, the babysitter's daily record of my newborn's activities, the doula's words of advice, hospital bills, to-do lists, and doodles I made while breastfeeding.

Materials

- Binder clips: ⅝" (1.6 cm) (2)
- Cardboard: 7" (17.8 cm) square
- Colored pencil: coordinating color
- Conservation tissue: 38" x 20' (96.5 cm x 6.1 m) machine-made Tengucho Thinnest
- Drafting tape
- Ephemera: 5" x 7" (12.7 x 17.8 cm) baby-themed notes (36); baby's hospital bracelet
- Pencil
- Thread: coordinating color
- Watercolor paints: shades of red (3)

Tools

- Mat knife
- Metal-edged ruler
- Needle
- Scissors
- Watercolor brush: ½" (1.3 cm)
- Yardstick

Instructions

Make the stencil

1. Mark the midpoints on all four sides of the cardboard square. Draw two lines connecting opposite midpoints, and two lines between opposite corners (see Fig. 1).

2. Using the drawn guidelines and ruler, cut the square vertically in half with the mat knife. Then cut the triangles and smaller squares (see Fig. 2). *Note: You will have an extra stencil each of shapes (a) and (c).*

Make the patches

3. Trace the shapes onto the backside of the baby notes and cut out, leaving a ¼" (.6 cm) margin around outlines. You will need 68 square patches, 24 large triangle patches, and 16 small triangle patches (see Fig. 3).

4. Paint the shapes with washes of watercolor paints, one shade of red per patch; let dry.

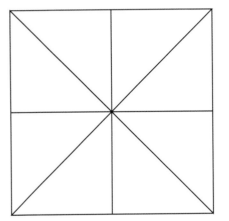

Fig. 1

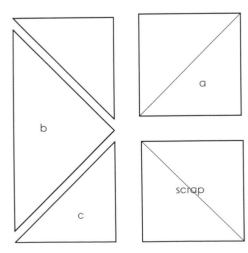

Fig. 2

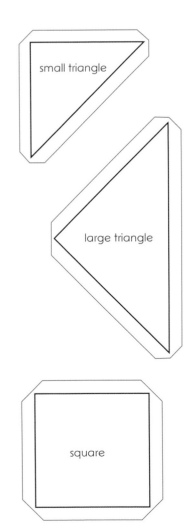

Fig. 3

Sew the quilt front

5. Sew the pieces into squares. Place two patches front-side facing, aligning the lines to be sewn together. Sew along the traced lines using a ½" (1.3 cm) long running stitch. You will need to make 13 A squares, four B squares, and eight C squares for a total of 25 (see Fig. 4).

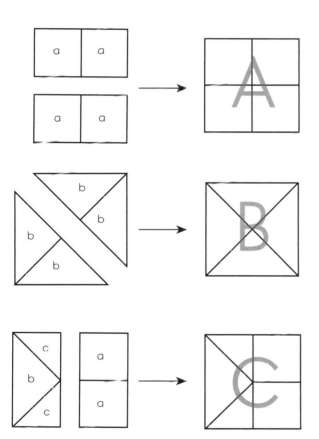

Fig. 4

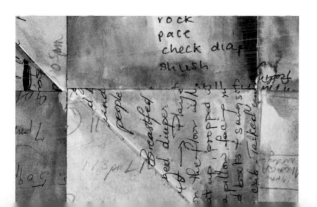

 Try This

Just about any kind of paper can be used in this quilt. I used my baby notes but there are a myriad of other possibilities—pages from an old passport, a filled notebook, bills or receipts, old sketches, playbills, paper money, gift wrap, an old book. Dig through memorabilia but keep in mind that the fibers in these types of paper are short and the shorter the paper fiber, the greater the possibility it will tear.

6. On a large, flat surface, lay out the squares in the pattern of the quilt (see Fig. 5) and begin to sew them together in the order shown (see Fig. 6). *Note: As the stitched pieces become larger, it helps to hold them together with drafting tape. If you were working in fabric, you would use pins, but because pins leave holes in paper, I use tape, which can be removed when the sewing is complete.*

A C A C A
C A B A C
A B A B A
C A B A A
A C A C A

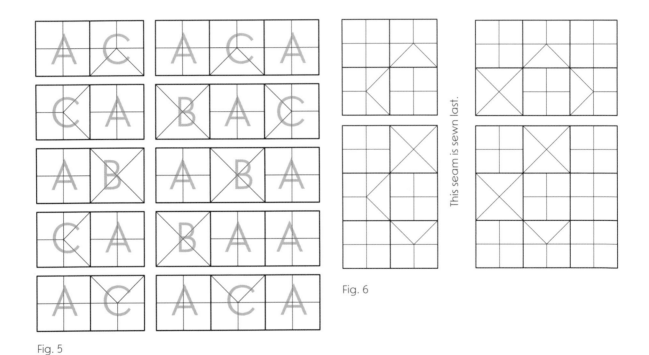

Fig. 5

This seam is sewn last.

Fig. 6

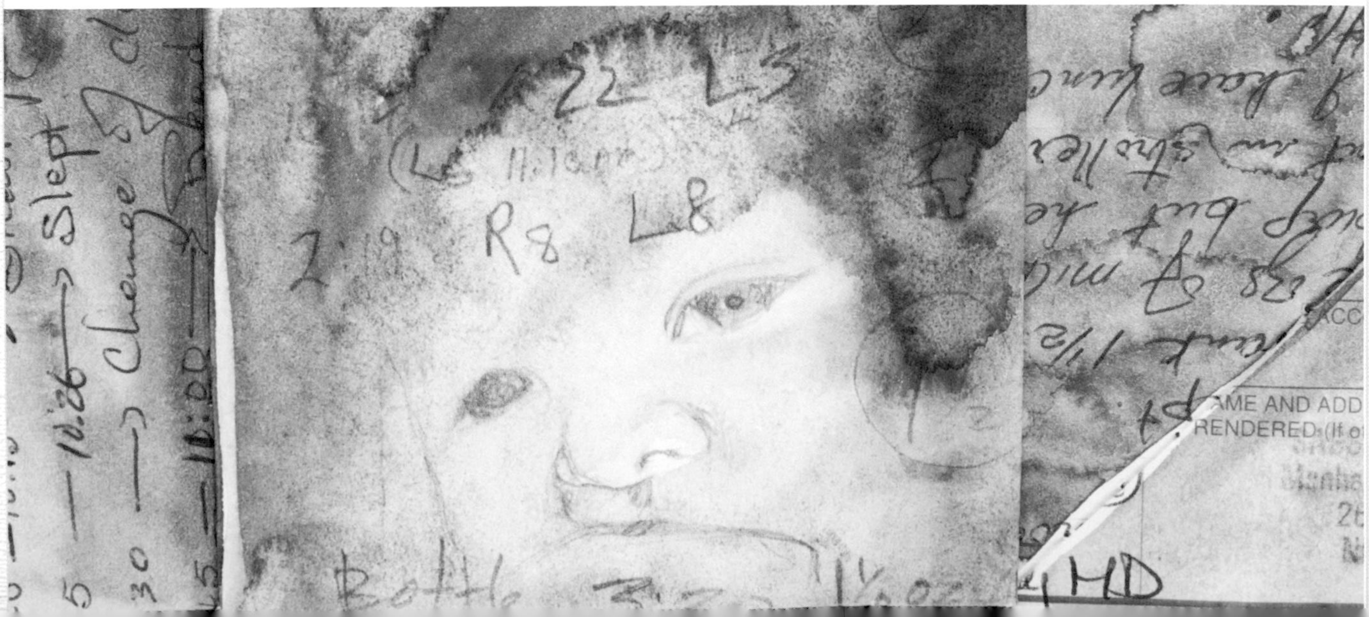

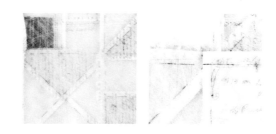

Back the quilt

7. Lay quilt face down on the Tengucho Thinnest tissue. Cut the tissue the same size or slightly larger than the quilt.

8. Draw a new line along the top edge of the quilt with the yardstick and a colored pencil. Secure the paper quilt to the backing with drafting tape. Sew the top-edge seam, following the new line.

9. With the quilt still face down, fold up all four edges of the paper quilt, including the top-edge seam. Remove the drafting tape.

10. Flip the quilt and backing so that the front side of the quilt faces outward and the quilt's backside is against the backing paper. Fold the edges of the backing so it lines up with the folded edges of the quilt. Stitch the remaining three edges together (see Fig. 7).

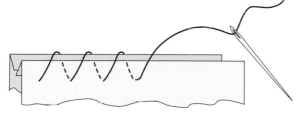

Fig. 7

Finish the quilt

11. Before completing the final seam along the last edge, sandwich the baby's hospital bracelet between the two papers and finish sewing closed.

12. Clamp the small binder clips along the top of the quilt to hang on the wall.

Embellishing a quilt with unusual elements like the baby's hospital ID bracelet adds an unexpected but very unique flair to a project. It's also a good way to save and display memorabilia that is difficult to work into a scrapbook page or diary.

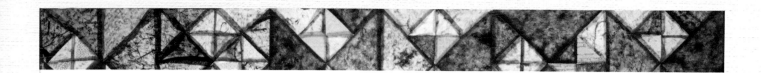

Family Quilt

Colleen Kong-Savage
60" x 61" (152.4 x 154.9 cm)

As a child, I moved from country to country before settling in New York City as an adult. This project is a celebration of home and community—things I found only after living in New York for a number of years.

I asked friends and family members to cover various handmade papers in handwriting. I also covered papers with my own writing. Graphology argues that one's personality is apparent in his or her handwriting. When I cut up the notes, the words can't be read in their original context, but the individuality of the writers' marks remain. That individual essence is what I wanted sewn into my "self-portraits"—after all, our identities are influenced by those around us.

Materials

- Cardboard: 7" (17.8 cm) square
- Drafting tape
- Papers: handmade approximately 25" x 37" (63.5 x 94 cm) assorted colors (15)
- Pencil
- Thread: coordinating color
- Water-soluble pens: coordinating colors
- Wooden dowel: ¾" (1.9 cm) (64" [162.6 cm])

Tools

- Kraft paper
- Mat knife
- Metal-edged ruler
- Needle
- Scissors
- Spray bottle of water (optional)

Instructions

Prepare the paper

Note: I used Thai papers of mulberry and unryu of various weights, as well as some papers from Nepal, Bhutan Tsasho, and India. Visit an art store that sells decorative papers in larger sizes.

1. Cut each large sheet of handmade paper into approximately 9" (22.9 cm) squares. Cover the papers in handwriting using water-soluble pens. *Note: Use your own handwriting or writing from family members, friends, co-workers, or neighbors. Give them the pens and ask them to write whatever they wish. If you like, spritz the writing with water to further obscure the handwriting. Note: Make sure you test how much the ink bleeds on the different papers before spraying the handwriting samples.*

2. Unfold the letters and lay them flat. If necessary, place them under a heavy book for a day to remove the folds.

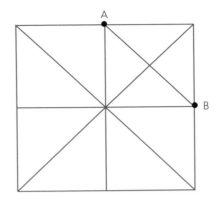

Fig. 1

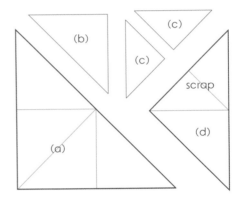

Fig. 2

Make the stencil

3. Mark the midpoints on all four sides of the cardboard square. Draw two lines connecting opposite midpoints, and two lines between opposite corners. Draw a line between midpoint A and midpoint B (see Fig. 1).

4. Cut out the stencil shapes using a mat knife and metal ruler, creating a stencil for a large triangle (a) and a medium triangle (b), and two stencils for a small triangle (c) (see Fig. 2).

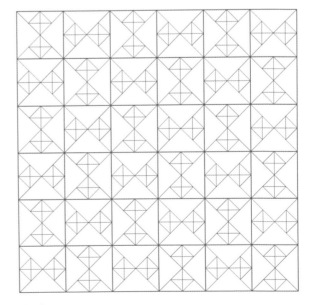

Fig. 3

5. When finished making the stencils and gathering the writing on the papers, use the diagram of the basic quilt pattern to design the quilt (see Fig. 3).

Make the patches

6. Lightly trace the triangles with pencil onto the backsides of the papers and then cut out, leaving a ¼" (.6 cm) margin around the outlines. You will need 72 big triangle patches (a), 144 medium triangles patches (b), and 288 small triangle patches (c) (see Fig. 4).

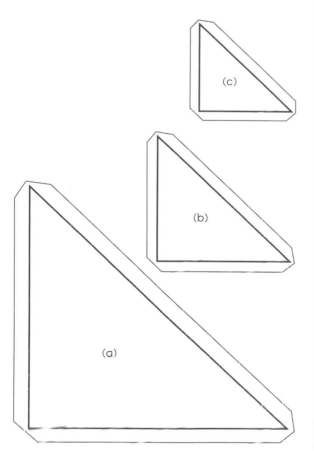

Fig. 4

Sew the quilt

7. Sew the triangles along the traced lines, following the configuration, to form a 10" (25.4 cm) basic square (see Figs. 5 and 6). Repeat to create 36 squares. *Note: If you like, varying the colors in different basic squares will give you some variety.*

8. Lay out all 36 squares on a clean, flat surface to decide how to compose the final quilt.

9. Sew the squares together. As the quilt gets larger and heavier, fasten the pieces together with drafting tape to make it easier to line them up. *Note: When the pieces get bigger, you may find it helpful to redraw the sewing lines.*

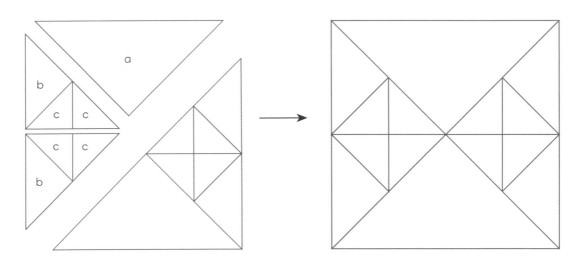

Fig. 5   Fig. 6

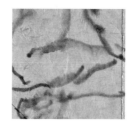
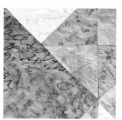

Variations on the basic quilt

Note: Because I wanted some asymmetry in my quilt, I incorporated many variations into the basic quilt pattern. I altered the arrangement of shapes in the basic square. Sometimes I incorporated the (d) triangle (see Fig. 2 on page 48) into the basic square. I played around with the seams, sometimes sewing pieces together so that the seams faced outward. I like the asymmetry because it emphasizes that there is a pattern that can be broken and the visible seams remind the viewer that this quilt is sewn.

Hanging the quilt

10. Cut a strip of kraft paper 40" (101.6 cm) long; the width should be the circumference of the wooden dowel plus 1" (2.5 cm). Cut this strip into thirds and fold each one in half lengthwise to create three hanging sleeves.

11. Space the folded sleeves evenly along the top edge of the quilt. Sew them on, leaving approximately a ¼"–½" (.6–1.3 cm) seam allowance (see Fig. 7). Thread the rod through the sleeves and hang to display.

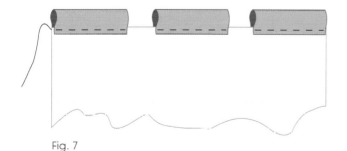

Fig. 7

✸ Try This

The papers and pens I used are not lightfast, meaning that they will fade over time, especially with exposure to light. This fact did not bother me because their transitory nature worked with my perception of community and home. To keep the original colors of your quilt, use pens with archival ink—but remember that they won't be water soluble or erasable. When finished, hang your quilt on walls with minimal sunlight.

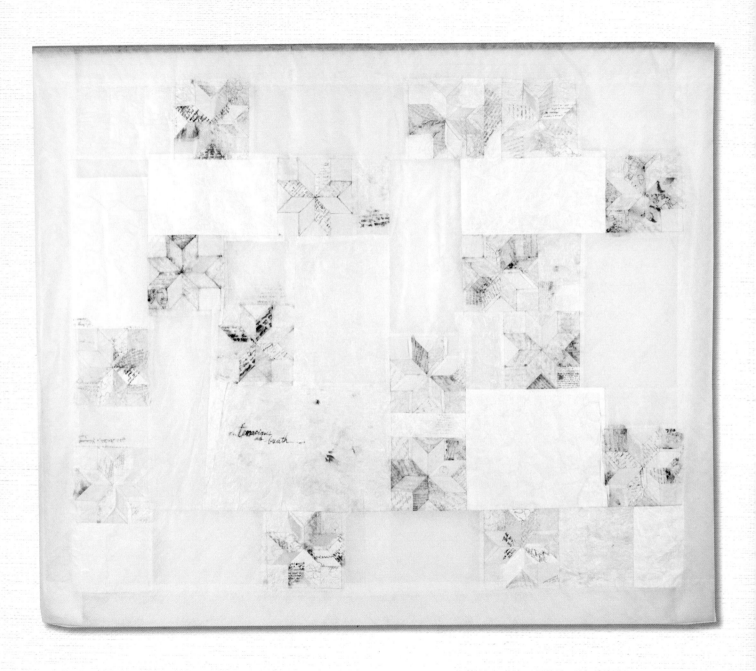

Women's Wishing Quilt

Colleen Kong-Savage
6' x 7' (1.83 x 2.13 m)

In creating this quilt, I was looking for a way to reach past my immediate community and tap into a larger group to which I belong—that of women in general. I wanted a project with the same generous spirit as Yoko Ono's Wishing Tree, where individuals are invited to write a wish on a tag and tie it to a small tree until the tree is covered with white papers.

For this project I asked several women to write down a wish for themselves and one for their mother or daughter. I also asked them to invite their mother or daughter to participate. This turned out to be more challenging than I anticipated—often for logistical reasons, but also due to the complexity of relationships. Many daughters were reluctant to share the project with their mothers, however the mothers seemed to have an easier time involving their daughters.

Materials

- Cardboard: 9" (22.9 cm) square
- Conservation tissue: 38" x 20' (96.5 cm x 6.1 m) machine-made Tengucho Thinnest
- Drafting tape
- Paper: handmade long-fiber approximately 25" x 37" (63.5 x 94 cm) assorted white (4)
- Pencil
- Pens: black ink
- Thread: coordinating colors
- Wooden dowel: 1" (2.5 cm) (7¼' [2.2 m])

Tools

- Mat knife
- Metal-edged ruler
- Scissors
- Sewing needle
- Straight pin
- Yardstick

Instructions

Paper Note

In this project I used papers from Thailand and Japan, mostly kozo, as well as some sulphite pulp. Many Asian papers are made from kozo fibers, which are from the inner bark of various mulberry plants. Sulphite is wood pulp that has been chemically treated to make it more suitable for papermaking. Everyday papers such as photocopier, notebook, and tracing paper are composed of short fibers and therefore are not as strong as long-fiber papers, which are more resistant to tearing. Visit an art store that sells decorative papers in larger sizes.

Make the stencils

1. Photocopy the Women's Wishing Quilt Patterns on page 123. Once pieced together, the shapes will form an approximate 8" (20.3 cm) square. Loosely tape the photocopy to the cardboard. Mark the corner of each shape with a hole or indentation using a straight pin and then remove the photocopy.

2. Connect the pinholes to recreate the square, triangle, and diamond using a pencil and ruler. Cut out the shapes with a mat knife and ruler. *Note: Use several light strokes with the mat knife instead of one heavy stroke. This makes cutting the board easier and gives you better control of the knife.*

Gather wishes

3. If your papers are large, cut them into more manageable sizes such as 8" x 10" (20.3 x 25.4 cm), or at least large enough to accommodate each stencil shape. Offer paper and a writing utensil to anyone you want to involve in this quilt. *Note: Ask individuals to make a wish for him or herself or someone else and have them write the wishes on one of your papers. Sometimes this is a challenge—wishes are personal, so sharing one requires openness and trust and some will want to take time to ponder it.* Once you have gathered enough wishes, you can begin making patches from them.

Make the basic square

4. On the backside of each sheet of wishes, lightly trace the cardboard stencils several times. Cut around the shapes, leaving a ¼" (.6 cm) margin outside the outlines. For each wishing star square you will need eight diamonds, four triangles, and four squares (see Fig. 1).

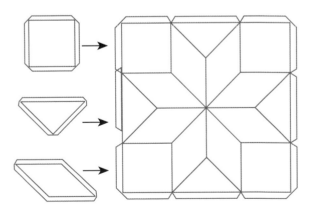

Fig. 1

5. Make one wishing star square by sewing the shapes together in the order shown (see Fig. 2). Place each shape front to

front and sew along the traced pencil lines. *Note: The illustrated shapes don't show the ¼" (.6 cm) seam allowance that you will have on the actual patches.*

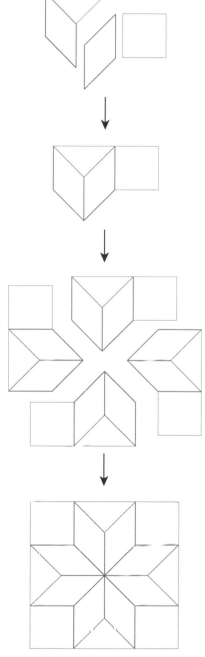

Fig. 2

6. Upon completing a square, use a ruler and colored pencil to draw a straight line along its four edges on the backside. Make as many wishing star squares as you want. *Note: I made 16 squares for this project.*

Assemble the quilt

7. Building the quilt is done rather organically. To get an idea of the quilt's final layout and size, arrange the finished squares into a large, loose shape with lots of space around each square.

8. Measure one side of a wishing star square. Trace the outline of a rectangle on the backside of a piece of white paper using a ruler and pencil. The long sides of this blank rectangle are the same length as the wishing star square (see Fig. 3). Cut out the rectangle so there is a ¼" (.6 cm) seam allowance outside the traced shape.

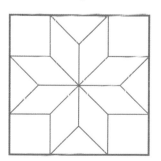

Fig. 3

9. Place the rectangle and wishing star square front to front, lining up the edges to be sewn. Following the pencil lines, sew the edge of the wishing star square to the edge of the blank rectangle to make a new rectangular unit. *Note: At this point you can either sew another wishing star square to the new unit on the opposite side of the rectangle or measure a side of this new unit and continue with the next step.*

10. Trace another rectangle on blank white paper. Again, at least one side of the drawn rectangle is the same length as the above unit (see Fig. 4). Cut out with the ¼" (.6 cm) seam allowance and sew along the lines. Repeat the steps with the remaining wishing star squares.

of both units are equal in length so the units will be flush when connected. Use a few pieces of drafting tape to hold the units together while sewing. *Note: It's a little like figuring out a puzzle and you can't be too rigid with the final pattern as you piece the quilt together. See Fig. 5 for two of many options for connecting three wishing star squares. The different order in which you piece together the squares and rectangles will affect the rectangle sizes and the order you sew them together.*

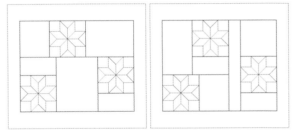

Fig. 5

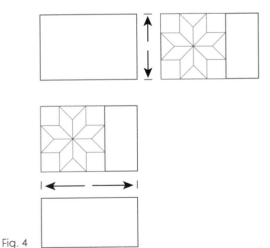

Fig. 4

11. Connect all of the units by surrounding the wishing star squares with rectangles of paper. The lengths of the rectangle's sides are determined by the lengths of the edge it will be sewn to. The edges

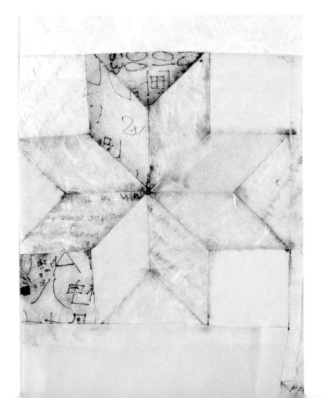

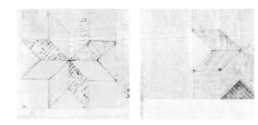

Back the quilt

12. Draw straight lines along all four edges of the rectangular quilt using a yardstick and pencil.

13. Cut the Tengucho Thinnest tissue the same size as the quilt. *Note: If the tissue is too small, stitch sheets together to achieve the necessary size.* Place the quilt on top of the backing, wrong sides together. Line up the edges of the two rectangles and hold everything in place with drafting tape.

14. Use a long running stitch to sew papers together. *Note: The line design of this stitch is up to you. I used a loose non-uniform swirling pattern, but you could also follow the outline of some rectangles through the quilt.* Remove the tape as you go along.

Finish the quilt

15. From the backing paper, cut two strips for the side borders. The length of the side border strips is equal to the quilt height and the width is equal to two times the desired border width plus 1" (2.5 cm).

16. Fold the two strips in half lengthwise. Sandwich about ½" (1.3 cm) of the quilt's edge between one of the folded strips, tape in place, and then sew; remove the tape.

17. Cut two more strips from the backing paper for the top and bottom borders. The length of the remaining border strips is equal to the quilt length plus four times the desired width of the side border. The width of the border strip is equal to two times the desired border width plus 1" (2.5 cm).

18. Fold in both ends of each strip so that the lengths equal the width of the quilt plus the side borders. Fold the strips in half lengthwise (see Fig. 6). Sandwich about ½" (1.3 cm) of the quilt's edge between one of the folded strips, tape in place, and then sew; remove the tape. The top border is also a hanging sleeve.

Hang the quilt

19. Cut the dowel to the length of the final quilt plus about 2" (5.1 cm) and thread it through the hanging sleeve.

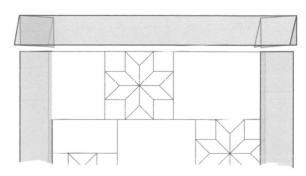

Fig. 6

Chapter 4

Incorporated Images

An image is a physical rendering of a person, thing, or even an idea that can range in complexity from a simple line drawing to a very detailed painting to a rubber stamp or photograph. Most of us have images that appear repeatedly in our work. They have special meaning to us in some way, whether it's a treasured memory or an image that simply appeals to us.

Sometimes images elicit a response because they call to mind an event or remind us of a certain scent or feeling. Colors and shapes play an important role in choosing images.

Use a collection of images to tell a story. They may all relate to a specific moment or perhaps they tell a story over a period of time. When it comes to designing your quilts, your image collection may include a variation of one particular subject with a particular theme or several different image subjects that portray a tale. You may even find that searching for images for a future paper quilt is just as fun as making the quilt itself.

In this chapter you'll see how the artists have incorporated a variety of different images into their work, from using a single image to several different images, as well as repeating images.

Red Paper Quilt Collage:
Little Blue Bird

Sunbonnet Sue Grows Up

Luna Quilt

Red Paper Quilt Collage: Little Blue Bird

Cathy Collier

8" x 10" (20.3 x 25.4 cm)

I was happily surprised to receive a package of vintage wallpaper in the mail from a paper swap partner. When I saw the pink and red pieces I knew I wanted to create a paper quilt. Once I found the stamps and discovered a handmade elephant sticker I had been given, the rest of the color palette fell into place. I drew the little blue bird, which added a personal element to the quilt.

Materials

- Adhesives: acid-free glue stick, decoupage medium
- Canvas board: 8" x 10" (20.3 x 25.4 cm)
- Cardstock: 8½" x 11" (21.6 x 27.9 cm) white
- Ephemera: labels, maps, paint chips, photos, stamps, wallpaper, wrapping paper
- Paint markers: coordinating colors
- Paper: catalogs, magazines, origami, tissue
- Pencil
- Photo corners
- Rolling ballpoint pen: extra-fine black
- Rub ons: letters, symbols
- Stickers

Tools

- Foam brush
- Metal-edged ruler
- Paper punches: circle ⅟₁₆" (.158 cm); ¼" (.6 cm); ½" (1.3 cm); ³⁄₁₆" (.476 cm) corner rounder
- Professional general-purpose drafting template
- Scissors

Instructions

Prepare the paper

1. Cut tissue paper into six 1½" x 8" (3.8 x 20.3 cm) and seven 1½" x 10" (3.8 x 25.4 cm) strips. These will be used to cover the canvas board and create the background.

Create the background

2. Pour approximately a tablespoon of decoupage medium directly onto one short side of the canvas board.

3. Cover the opposite side of the board with a thin coat of decoupage medium using a foam brush.

4. Carefully, but quickly, lay the strips of tissue paper across the canvas board and lightly brush decoupage medium over each piece. *Note: Spreading the decoupage medium thinly will prevent the tissue paper from tearing or bubbling.* Lay down the 8" (20.3 cm) strips first and then layer the 10" (25.4 cm) strips over these in a grid or basketweave pattern; let dry.

Make the arrangement

5. Cut a 2¼" (5.7 cm) square and a 2" x 2¼" (5.1 x 5.7 cm) rectangle from cardstock to use as templates. Cut out quilting squares from vintage wallpaper samples or wrapping paper using the templates. Cut nine rectangles and three small squares for a total of twelve pieces per quilt.

6. Round the edges of some of the quilting pieces with the ³⁄₁₆" (.476 cm) corner rounder. *Note: I like to keep the corners on some of the pieces but you may want to round all of the corners.*

7. Attach the quilting pieces to the canvas board in a pattern of four rows of three pieces using a glue stick. *Note: One of each of the three smaller squares should be incorporated into each row of four so all of the pieces fit.* Let the glue dry thoroughly before continuing.

8. Trace two 1" (2.5 cm) hexagons and two 1¼" (3.2 cm) hexagons onto origami, found paper, or ephemera of your choice using the general-purpose drafting template. Mat each hexagon on a complementary piece of paper and cut out. Glue each set onto two separate squares.

9. Embellish the various quilt pieces with stickers, ephemera, rub ons, and paper shapes punched from coordinating papers, reserving one large piece.

10. Lightly sketch a simple bird on the reserved piece. Draw over the pencil lines with the rolling ballpoint pen to create clean edges. Use the paint markers to fill in the drawing.

Finish the quilt

11. Spread a very small amount of decoupage medium over the dry completed piece to preserve and enhance the color of the project.

Blue Paper Quilt Collage: A Winter's Delight

Variation of Red Paper Quilt Collage: Little Blue Bird

Wintertime is my favorite season. I look forward to the way the light changes in the winter. Trees are dark shapes outlined in silver. Snow falls, covering the landscape in glitter. I love how the wind blows and chills you to the bone, but the warmth indoors is incredibly cozy and romantic. It doesn't always snow where I live so this quilt is a wonderful way of bringing the delight of winter to my warm sunny locale.

Sunbonnet Sue Grows Up

Terri Stegmiller

16" (40.6 cm) square

My mother made me a Sunbonnet Sue quilt for my bed when I was young. I enjoy drawing female faces and using them in my art. One day I decided it was time for Sue to grow up and that thought sparked the idea for this paper quilt.

Materials

- Acrylic paint: assorted colors
- Adhesive: temporary
- Fabric: 16" (40.6 cm) square
- Fabric-backed paper: 16" (40.6 cm) square
- Fusible web: 16" (40.6 cm) square (2)
- Heavyweight interfacing: 16" (40.6 cm) square
- Inkpad: black
- Paper: 8½" x 11" (21.6 x 27.9 cm) assorted coordinating colors and patterns (4–5)
- Pencil
- Thread: coordinating colors
- Watercolor paper: 8½" x 11" (21.6 x 27.9 cm) white

Tools

- Iron and ironing surface
- Metal-edged ruler
- Paintbrush
- Scissors
- Sewing machine
- Template plastic

Instructions

Prepare the image

1. Practice drawing the image you wish to have on your quilt to fit in a 6" (15.2 cm) square. Once you're happy with the image, trace it onto the watercolor paper.

2. Paint the image with acrylic paints; let dry. Trim the image to 6" (15.2 cm) square.

The pattern and colors on the quilt back support the design on the front while also making the hanging sleeve seem to disappear when the rod is removed.

Prepare the paper

3. Fuse the fabric-backed paper to the interfacing to create the background.

4. Draw the flowers and their centers freehand on your choice of paper and cut them out. *Note: To save the shapes for use in another quilt, draw them on template plastic, cut out, and trace onto the desired papers.*

5. Cut twenty-seven 1½" (3.8 cm) squares of papers in assorted colors.

6. Lightly rub the edges of each of the paper squares with the black inkpad to distress them.

Make the arrangement

7. Cut a 7" (17.8 cm) square piece of paper to frame the image. Center the image over the frame paper and secure with temporary adhesive. Straight stitch ⅛" (.3 cm) from the edge of the image with a coordinating thread.

8. Position the flowers and flower centers and secure with temporary adhesive. Free-motion straight stitch with a coordinating thread. Paint, draw, or stitch flower stems.

9. Place the image on the background and arrange the paper squares around it. When you are satisfied with the arrangement, secure the pieces in place with temporary adhesive.

10. Zigzag stitch around the frame with a coordinating thread.

11. Free-motion straight stitch the squares with a contrasting thread.

Finish the quilt

12. Create a hanging sleeve, if desired, following the directions on page 23. Attach the sleeve to the fabric.

13. Fuse the fabric to the back of the interfacing, making certain the hanging sleeve is at the top of the quilt.

14. Zigzag stitch around the entire quilt, making sure to include the top edge of the hanging sleeve, if there is one. *Note: The recommended stitch width is 4–5 mm and the stitch length is .4–.8 mm but these may need to be adjusted, depending on the thickness of the thread used.*

Try This

A simple sketched image would look nice if you prefer not to paint your image. I find that incorporating some black elements with bright colors really helps the colors pop.

Luna Quilt

Zana Clark
13" x 16" (33 x 40.6 cm)

This project was not planned in the traditional sense of following an artistic structure. It was the result of collecting a number of favorite samples I had created in demonstrations at a long string of conventions I was attending at the time. After collecting the samples and arranging them on a black mat board I created step-by-step instructions so the finished quilt could be taught as a class. The beauty of this "un-process" lies in its diverse, yet similar, patterns of color, texture, and imagery that created this wonderful water-colored piece of art.

Materials

- Bleach pen
- Colored pencils: various colors
- Double-sided tape
- Inkpad: black permanent
- Mat board: 13" x 16" (33 x 40.6 cm) black core
- Sprayable watercolors: coordinating colors (6–8)
- Watercolor paper: 140# cold press 4" x 5½" (10.2 x 14 cm) (9)

Tools

- Heat tool
- Plastic stencils: fern, polyester sequin film, snowflake
- Rubber stamp: luna moth
- Water cup
- Watercolor brush: #8 round

Instructions

Prepare the image

1. Stamp the luna moth once on each piece of watercolor paper using the black permanent inkpad, varying the direction and placement of the image to add visual interest. Dry each stamped piece with a heat tool.

Color the image

2. Cover the entire surface of one of the stamped paper pieces using three different sprayable watercolors. Using a sweeping motion, spray one color over the top third of the paper. *Note: If you get splatters or splotches, spray the area again.* Spray a second color, slightly overlapping the first color, filling the middle third of the paper. Repeat to fill the bottom third of the paper with a third color. Repeat on the remaining watercolor pieces, varying the colors and the angle of the paper as desired.

3. Place a plastic stencil on the surface of one of the painted paper pieces. Spray a coordinating color over the stencil using a sweeping motion. Carefully remove the stencil and dry the paper surface with the heat tool. *Note: You can place a different stencil on the paper surface and select another color and spray again. As long as the paper is dry the colors won't bleed and the images will be clear. Repeat using the stencils on the remaining paper pieces.*

 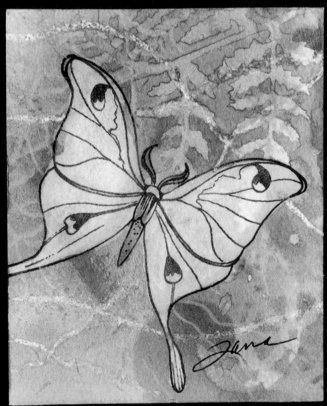

Add visual texture

4. Add visual texture to any or all of the stenciled paper pieces using a bleach pen to remove areas of color. *Note: Because the images have been stamped in permanent ink, the bleach will only lift the color, not the ink.*

5. Apply water with a watercolor brush in lines or splatters, or paint inside the stamped image to lighten any color. *Note: Always let water sit on the color for at least a minute and then remove the excess moisture by blotting with a paper towel.*

6. Color around or inside the stamped or stenciled images to accent areas, or scribble over the painted background with colored pencils as desired.

Assemble the quilt

7. Adhere each paper quilt piece to the mat board using double-sided tape, leaving a ⅛" (.3 cm) border around each piece.

✳ Try This

Make a version of a crazy quilt by starting with a single 12" x 18" (30.5 x 45.7 cm) sheet of watercolor paper. Randomly stamp eight to ten moth images in permanent ink on the paper. Turn the paper over and cut it into approximately eight to ten straight-edged pieces. Number them on the back in order; this will make it easier to put your puzzle pieces back together. Continue with the techniques in the project instructions to complete the quilt. Mount the pieces on a black 13" x 19" (33 x 48.3 cm) mounting board, leaving a ¼" (.6 cm) gap between each puzzle piece.

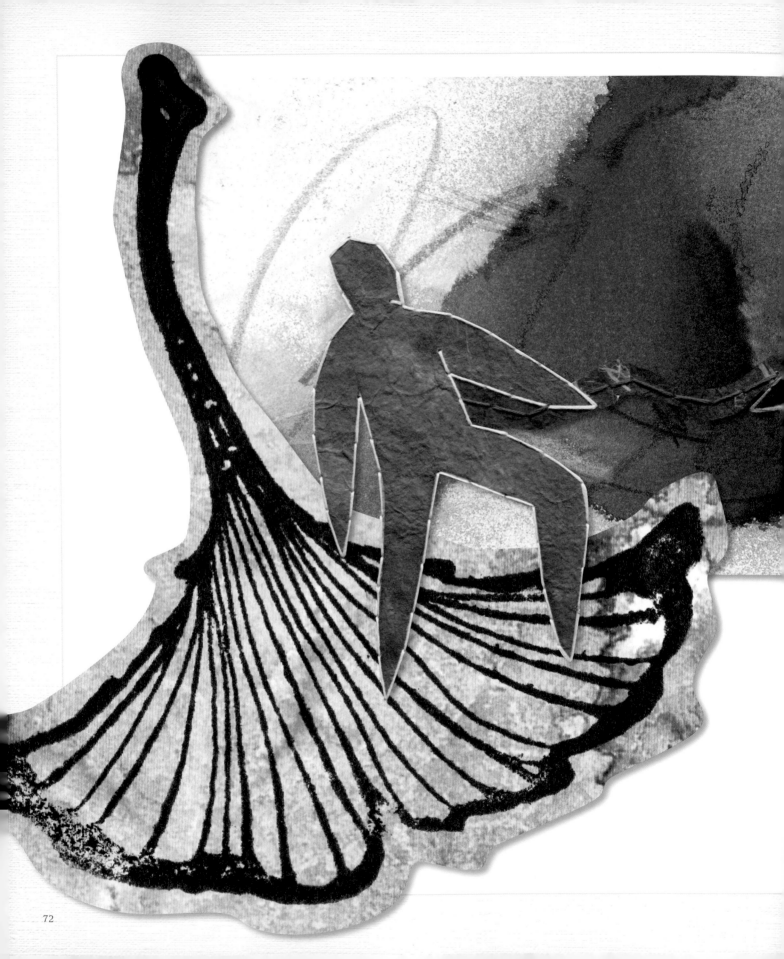

Chapter 5
Art Quilts

Art is defined as the conscious use of skill and creative imagination, especially in the production of aesthetic objects. Art quilts run the gamut of quilting techniques, often incorporating several types such as traditional, appliqué, and painting, into one piece of work. It seems that more often art quilters are bringing their art education and design principals to the quilting arena and creating works that are sometimes referred to as contemporary art. That term encompasses a wide range of styles from abstract to pictorial.

An abstract quilt typically focuses on the use of colors and form and may or may not represent real objects. One of the things I truly enjoy about abstract art quilts is that as the viewer I can interpret the piece in my own way.

Pictorial quilts usually portray a picture, scene, or image. When making a pictorial art quilt the artist may be portraying a scenic view, remembering an image from childhood, or sharing thoughts about a worldly matter that has affected him or her.

No matter which style of art quilting you prefer, you will find that combining art and paper quilts is extremely easy and quite enjoyable. The artists in this chapter have truly created paper quilts with skill and imagination, producing beautiful works of art.

Follow the Leader
Abstract Quilt
Shared Home
Kimono Sphere Quilt
Tug of War and Peace

Follow the Leader

Carol White
11½" (29.2 cm) square

This paper quilt represents the diversity found throughout the world. Each figure has its own identity indicated by its color, suggesting that all humans share the same needs and wants. All of the figures are moving forward as they follow the lead of one figure. The angular and geometric lines of the stitched shapes contrast the natural elements of the plant images, indicating the struggle between natural and manmade environments.

Materials

- Acrylic paint: ultramarine blue, white
- Decoupage medium
- Drawing paper
- Embroidery floss: assorted colors (5)
- Handmade paper: 8½" x 11" (21.6 x 27.9 cm) assorted transparent colors (9); opaque color (1)
- Watercolor paper: 11½" (29.2 cm) square heavyweight

Tools

- Art eraser
- Artist paintbrushes: 1" (2.5 cm) flat acrylic brush; assorted as desired
- Craft knife
- Digital camera and printer
- Metal-edged ruler
- Pencil
- Quilter's T-pin
- Scissors
- Thimble
- Upholstery needle

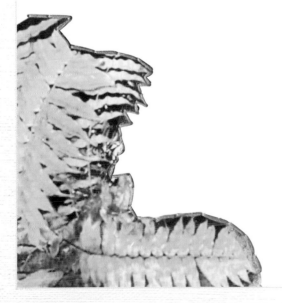

Instructions

Create the patterns

1. Create a sketch or drawing of the theme of the work. *Note: This step is not necessary if you choose to work in a more freeform manner.* Use the Art Figure Pattern on page 123 to create figures for the project. To create a mirror-image figure, simply flip over the pattern and trace as desired.

2. Draw shapes, patterns, or figures on the drawing paper and then cut them out.

Create the design

3. Trace the shapes onto handmade paper and cut out the pieces.

4. Arrange the pieces on the watercolor paper until you are happy with the design. Take a digital photo of the composition to record the final design and print it out for reference as you assemble the project.

5. Working in sections, apply the decoupage medium to the watercolor paper using the 1" (2.5 cm) brush. Attach the paper pieces to the watercolor paper following the reference photo. Smooth each paper piece after adhering it to the project to ensure that no bubbles form underneath.

6. After the entire work is dry, use the metal-edged ruler and craft knife to trim any stray pieces of handmade paper that extend beyond the edges of the piece.

Embellish the design

7. Accent the blue sky using a mixture of ultramarine blue and white paint and an assortment of artist's brushes. This creates varied textures on the surface of the piece and unique contrasts between the background and the figures. *Note: Be sure to wait until all of the figures and background surface are completely dry before adding the acrylic paint touches.*

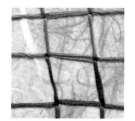

Finish the quilt

8. Determine which areas of the work you will stitch around and then pierce holes along the lines using the quilter's T-pin. *Note: Be careful not to tear the paper.*

9. Sew under and over through the pierced areas of the design using different embroidery threads as desired, the upholstery needle, and a running stitch. *Note: When the thread runs out, knot the end and trim the excess. Tie a single knot at the end of the new thread and come up from underneath the project in the next pierced hole. After reaching the end of one line, turn the thread in the opposite direction and complete an over-under pattern creating a continuous, unbroken line (see Fig. 1). The final sewn work will look like a series of dashes.*

10. Check the back of the finished piece and trim any stray threads.

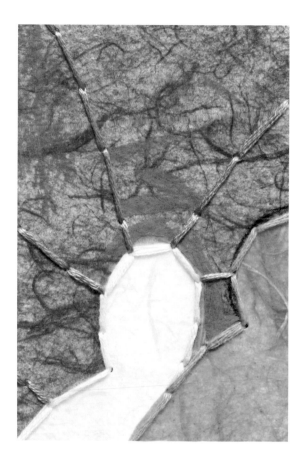

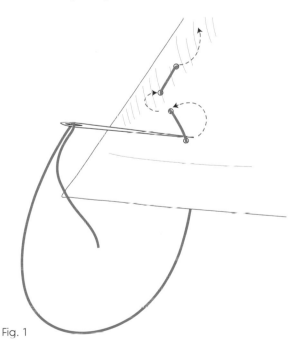

Fig. 1

Try This

If your work bows or bends due to the wetness of the paint on the paper, place the completed dry piece between two heavy books for several hours to flatten it.

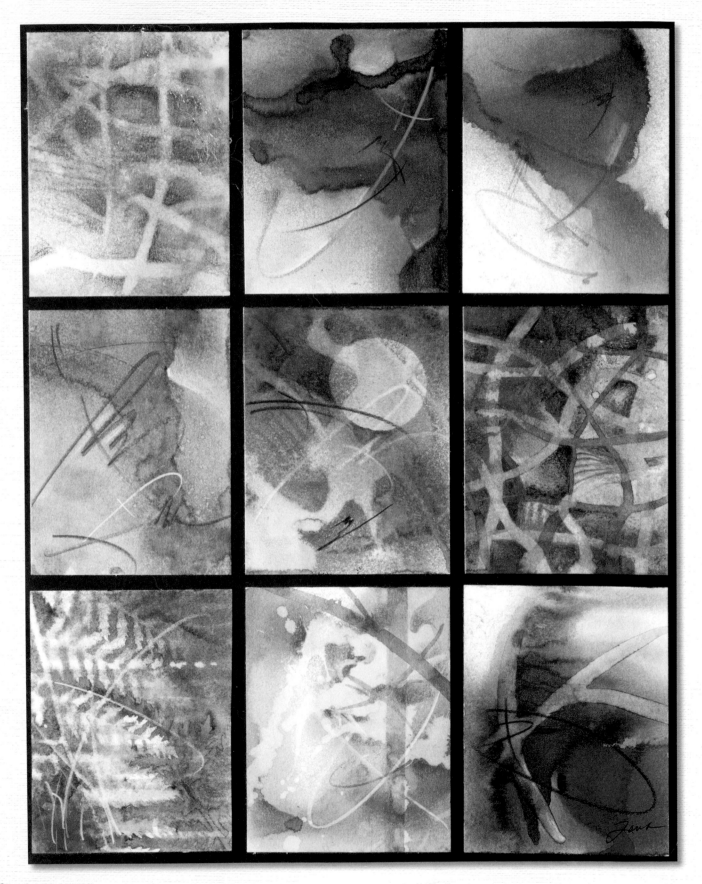

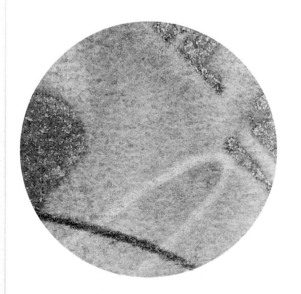

Abstract Quilt

Zana Clark
12½" x 16" (31.8 x 40.6 cm)

This project incorporates nine pieces using four different techniques to create an artsy abstract grid. Use water to encourage bleeding, feathering, and mixing of the liquid watercolors. Treat each paper piece as a mini-painting. By combining these techniques and playing with water you will learn how easy it is to create and manipulate water media and invent your own techniques.

Materials

- Adhesive: double-sided tape
- Fine-point marker: black
- Liquid sprayable watercolors: coordinating colors (12)
- Mat board: 12½" x 16" (31.8 x 40.6 cm) black
- Watercolor paper: 4" x 5" (10.2 x 12.7 cm) 140# cold press (9)

Tools

- Heat tool
- Paper towels
- Plastic circle template: 1" (2.5 cm)
- Plastic plant leaves
- Spray bottle with water
- Water cup
- Watercolor brush: #8 round

Instructions

Technique note

Because each piece is unique, experiment with the following four techniques to create nine different paintings. Always allow the piece to dry thoroughly before adding it to the quilt.

Prepare the paper

1. Spray or brush watercolors on some of the watercolor papers as desired and then dry with a heat tool. Reserve the remaining papers for the Water Works and the Water Resist techniques.

Water Works technique

2. Note: This is a wet-on-wet technique. Spray the watercolor paper surface lightly with water and then spray a liquid watercolor on a section. Tilt and turn the paper to allow the color to run. Add a second and third color, tilting and turning the paper to allow the colors to bleed into each other. When you find the color arrangement pleasing, dry the piece with the heat tool to stop further blending.

Water Lift technique

3. Using the watercolor brush and water, paint over areas on one of the painted watercolor papers to lighten or remove the colors. Try splattering or throwing water loaded on the brush tip or brush over a painted area using very wet strokes. Let the water sit on the paper surface for a minute and then gently blot with a paper towel.

Water Resist technique

4. Paint water lines or shapes on a dry watercolor paper surface. Spray liquid watercolor over the paper surface and then gently dry with a heat tool. Using a paper towel, blot off any excess water. Repeat this step as many times as you like to create layers of textures and colors.

Masking technique

5. Create a stencil using geometric shapes cut from cardboard, the plastic circle template, and plastic plant leaves, or

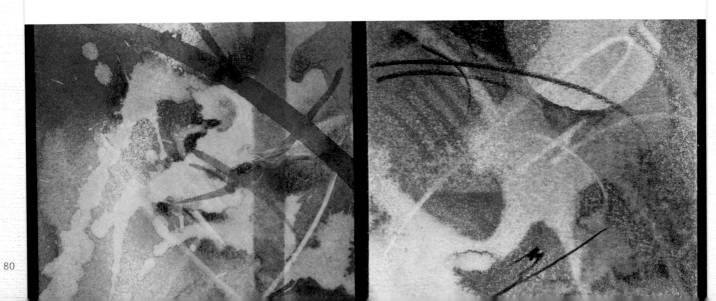

experiment with other objects from around the house. Cover a section of a painted watercolor paper with the desired stencil and spray the paper with a coordinating watercolor. Move or change the stencil and repeat this process using another water-color to create various layers of patterns and textures as desired. Be sure to dry with a heat tool after adding each color.

Assembling the quilt

6. Arrange the mini-paintings on the mat board in a pleasing arrangement of color, texture, and movement. Adhere the pieces to the mat board in a grid pattern using double-sided tape and then sign and date the quilt with the black marker.

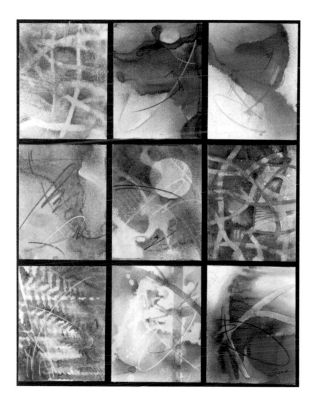

 Try This

Accent an area or detail or add additional textures with colored pencil and chalk applications to complete the mini paintings. Study each painted paper piece to see where an extra zip can be incorporated. I especially like to use white and black pencils to accentuate the lightest and darkest values in each piece. I added a bit of glitz to one of the paintings by ironing on a small piece of fusible iridescent fiber after the piece had dried.

Map of Techniques Used
#1 Water Works
#2 Water Lift
#3 Water Resist
#4 Masking

Top Row:
Left used #1 and #2
Middle used #1
Right used #1

Middle Row:
Left used #1
Middle used #1, #3, and #4
Right used #1 and #2

Bottom Row:
Left used #1 and #4
Middle used #1 and #3
Right used #1 and #2

Shared Home

Carol White
11 ½" (29.2 cm) square

///

Shared Home acknowledges the importance of our shared planet. The house represents the earth with each figure connected even though they stand on opposite sides of the building. The mirror images are quite intentional and serve as symbols of humanity. They remind us that regardless of race or geographic location, all people share the same potential to contribute to a better world or to separate themselves into groups. Each figure reaches toward the other and touches the house as if circling the planet in a rhythmic dance.

Materials

- Acrylic gel medium
- Acrylic paint: assorted colors (5); black
- Decoupage medium
- Drawing paper
- Embroidery floss (11)
- Handmade paper: 8½" x 11" (21.6 x 27.9 cm) assorted transparent colors (10)
- Ric-rac: 5¼" (13.3 cm) yellow (2)
- Watercolor paper: 11½" (29.2 cm) square heavyweight

Tools

- Art eraser
- Craft knife
- Digital camera and printer
- Metal-edged ruler
- Paintbrush. 1" (2.5 cm) flat
- Pencil
- Quilter's T-pin
- Scissors
- Upholstery needle

Instructions

Create the patterns

1. Create a sketch or drawing of the theme of the work as desired. *Note: This step is not necessary if you choose to work in a more freeform manner.*

2. Draw shapes, patterns, or figures on the drawing paper and then cut them out.

Create the design

3. Create the mirror images using the Art Figure Pattern on page 123. Stack two sheets of handmade paper on top of each other and trace the figure on the top sheet and then cut both papers together to ensure that the figures are the same size. Flip one of the figures over so they are facing each other.

4. Create the house shape by cutting a 2¼" x 9" (5.7 x 22.9 cm) rectangular piece of handmade paper and then trim the corners off one of the short ends for the top of the house. Cut four ¾" x 1" (1.9 x 2.5 cm) rectangles from a coordinating color of handmade paper for the windows and adhere down the center of the rectangle. Cut a ½" x 1½" (1.3 x 3.8 cm) piece for the door and adhere at the bottom of the rectangle.

5. Trace the shapes onto the desired handmade papers and cut out the pieces. Opaque papers can be used in some sections and transparent in others. *Note: Dark purple paper was used to create a wave border at the bottom of the project to ground the whole piece.*

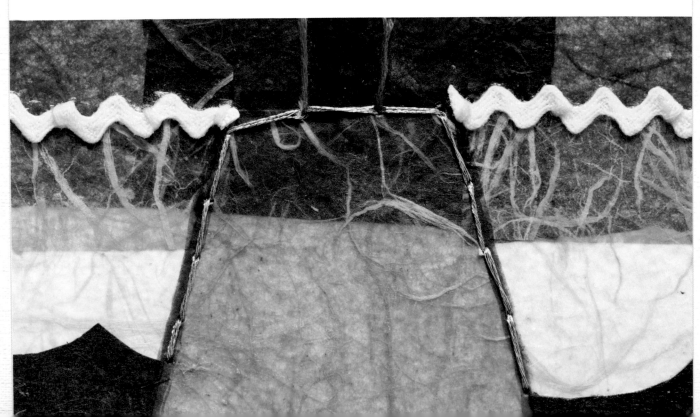

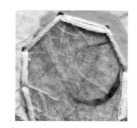

6. Arrange the pieces on the watercolor paper until you are happy with the design. Take a digital photo of the composition and print it out for reference as you assemble the project.

7. Working in sections, apply decoupage medium to the watercolor paper using the 1" (2.5 cm) brush. Attach the paper pieces to the watercolor paper following the reference photo. Smooth each paper piece after adhering it to the project to ensure that no bubbles form underneath.

8. After the entire work is dry, use the metal-edged ruler and craft knife to trim any stray pieces of handmade paper that extend beyond the edges of the piece.

Embellish the design

9. Sew the two pieces of ric-rac to the paper on either side of the building using embroidery floss and the upholstery needle. Cover the ric-rac with acrylic gel medium; let dry.

10. Accent the top and right sides of the windows with black paint to create the illusion of three-dimensional space. *Note: The zigzag patterns are repeated throughout the work and contrast the curved spirals at the top of the work.*

Finish the quilt

11. Determine which areas of the work you will stitch around and then pierce holes along the lines using the quilter's T-pin.

12. Sew under and over through the pierced areas of the design using different embroidery threads as desired, the upholstery needle, and a running stitch. *Note: When the thread runs out, knot the end and trim off the excess. Tie a single knot in the end of the new thread and come up from underneath the project in the next pierced hole. After reaching the end of one line, turn the thread in the opposite direction and complete an over-under pattern, creating a continuous, unbroken line. The final sewn work will look like a series of dashes.*

13. Check the back of the finished piece and trim any stray threads.

 Try This

Lay transparent papers on top of each other and hold them up to the light to help you determine how the colors will change when they are adhered together on a project. Experiment with several layers to achieve different intensities and visual depth.

Kimono Sphere Quilt

Zana Clark
10" x 16" (25.4 x 40.6 cm)

The inspiration for this quick and simple quilt project happened while I was searching through a pile of stamped samples for an element to add to another project. I discovered this kimono image and imagined it against a geometric background of patterned paper, but when I laid the stamped piece on top of a variety of art papers nothing quite spoke to me. All the papers felt overpowering so I chose two subtle art papers and cut them into squares and rectangles. I pieced the paper shapes together to create a geometric grid background and laid the stamped image on top as the perfect finishing touch.

Materials

- Adhesives: hot glue gun and glue sticks, repositionable mounting adhesive
- Bamboo stick: 10" (25.4 cm)
- Cardstock: glossy black, glossy white
- Inkpads: black permanent, dye-based coordinating colors (3–4)
- Mounting board: 10" x 16" (25.4 x 40.6 cm)
- Papers: 10" x 16" (25.4 x 40.6 cm) coordinating colors (2)
- Quilting bias tape: black (8" [20.3 cm])
- Wax-based crayons: coordinating colors (5–6)

Tools

- Cotton squares
- Heat tool
- Metal-edged ruler
- Rubber stamps: 2½" x 3" (6.4 x 7.6 cm) ginkgo leaf; 4" x 4½" (10.2 x 11.4 cm) ginkgo leaf; 5½" (14 cm) kimono sphere stamp
- Scissors

Instructions

Prepare the Paper

1. Cut each of the two sheets of paper into eight 4" x 5" (10.2 x 12.7 cm) rectangles. Choose four rectangles of each color and reserve the rest for another project. Apply the repositionable mounting adhesive to the paper sections and rub to ensure a secure bond. Trim each piece carefully before peeling off the protective backing. *Note: I cut one of each of the coordinating paper sections in half to mix up the predictable pattern, using half of each art paper to complete one 4" x 5" (10.2 x 12.7 cm) square.* Alternately arrange each paper section onto the mounting board and burnish from the top surface. The pattern will be two 4" x 5" (10.2 x 12.7 cm) paper sections across and four 4" x 5" (10.2 x 12.7 cm) paper sections down.

2. Stamp a cascading pattern of large and small ginkgo leaf stamps in permanent ink over the paper quilt background. Dry with a heat tool.

Create the medallion

3. Scribble lines on the surface of the white cardstock using crayons as desired.

4. Rub a cotton square directly on one of the dye-based inkpads. Apply the color to the cardstock, rubbing in a firm, circular motion and covering the crayon lines. Repeat this color application, using a

clean cotton square for each new color. *Note: Make sure to overlap the colors but don't worry about going outside the edge of the image because it will be trimmed off.*

5. Stamp the kimono sphere in permanent ink over the colored scribbled lines. Dry with a heat tool, which causes the crayon to melt into the paper and become permanent.

6. Trim excess paper around the stamped image. Mount the piece onto the black cardstock and trim, leaving a ½" (1.3 cm) border around the image.

Assemble the quilt

7. Adhere the matted piece to the mounted paper quilt, positioning it in the upper third of the board using the hot glue gun.

8. Cut the black bias tape in half. Fold each piece in half, forming 2" (5.1 cm) loops, and hot glue them on the center top back of the mounting board. Thread a bamboo stick through the loops to hang the quilt.

 Try This

I buy and hoard a lot of beautiful papers. I'm afraid that if I use a special piece, I'll never be able to find it again—so I save it, which translates into more hoarding. I could open my own paper store, but I won't because I'd have to part with too many pieces. I love to look at beautiful papers, touch them, and think about all the wonderful things I could do with each piece, but I won't because of my hoarding problem. My solution is to cut special pieces of art paper in half. I keep a stash of the saved halves in a designated paper drawer. The other halves go into another drawer for use in a project. This way I have given myself permission to use and play with all my special papers.

Tug of War and Peace

Carol White

11 ½" (29.2 cm) square

This project illustrates the link between elements always present during
times of war or conflict. The branches
stand between the two figures to serve
as barriers. However, the red line, or
bloodline, reaches beyond the branches
to touch each person. The message is
that as human beings there are parts of
one another we will never understand
because of our differences. Whether we
face language barriers or cultural misun-
derstandings, or are separated by physical obstacles, humans continue to battle
one another for space. But for all people
everywhere, our blood is red. In the end,
beyond the chaos of everyday life, the
ideal is a peaceful existence.

Materials

- Acrylic paint: orange, red
- Adhesives: decoupage medium, masking tape
- Drawing paper
- Embroidery floss: assorted colors (6)
- Ephemera: 4¾" x 1" (12.1 x 2.5 cm) fern photo (2)
- Gesso: black
- Handmade paper: 8½" x 11" (21.6 x 27.9 cm) assorted colors and patterns (7)
- Watercolor paper: 11½" (29.2 cm) square heavyweight

Tools

- Art eraser
- Craft knife
- Digital camera and printer
- Metal-edged ruler
- Paintbrush: 1" (2.5 cm) flat
- Pencil
- Quilter's T-pin
- Scissors
- Upholstery needle

Instructions

Create the pattern

1. Create a sketch or drawing of the theme of the work. *Note: This step is not necessary if you choose to work in a more freeform manner.* Use the Art Figure Pattern on page 123 to create figures for the project. To create a mirror-image figure, simply flip the pattern over and trace as desired.

2. Draw shapes, patterns, or figures on the drawing paper; cut out.

3. Create the outer sections of the background with the turquoise patterned handmade paper. *Note: The curved patterns of the patterned paper were selected to contrast with the geometric, angled lines in the center of the project.*

Create the design

4. Trace the shapes onto the handmade paper and cut out the pieces.

5. Arrange the pieces on the watercolor paper until you are happy with the design. Take a digital photo of the completed composition to record the final design and print it out for reference as you assemble the project.

6. Mask the outside of a 2¼" (5.7 cm) section in the center of the watercolor paper with masking tape. Paint the center area with black gesso and the artist's brush of your choice to create contrast for the fern leaves; let dry.

7. Working in sections, apply the decoupage medium to the watercolor paper

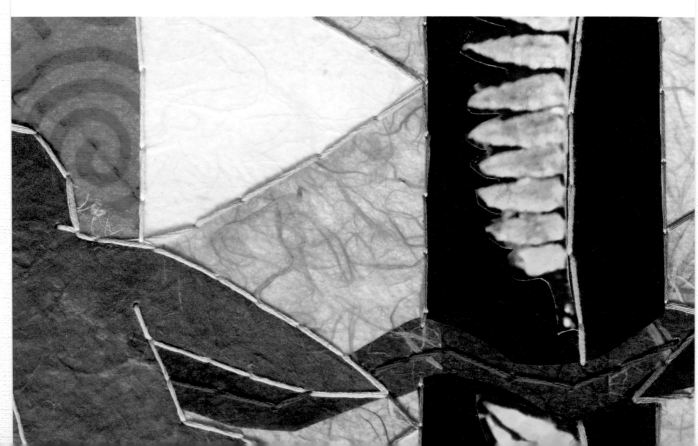

using the 1" (2.5 cm) brush. Attach the paper pieces to the watercolor paper following the reference photo. Smooth each paper piece after adhering it to the project to ensure that no bubbles form underneath.

8. After the entire work is dry, use the ruler and craft knife to trim any stray pieces of handmade paper that extend beyond the edges of the piece.

Embellish the design

9. Adhere the fern images in the center section of the quilt.

10. Paint a ¼" (.6 cm) red border around the outside edge of the watercolor paper. Add touches of orange acrylic paint as desired; let dry.

Finish the quilt

11. Determine which areas of the work you will stitch around and then pierce holes along the lines using the quilter's T-pin. *Note: Be careful not to tear the paper.*

12. Sew under and over through the pierced areas of the design using different embroidery threads as desired, the upholstery needle, and a running stitch. *Note: When the thread runs out, knot the end and trim off the excess. Tie a single knot in the end of the new thread and come up from underneath the project in the next pierced hole. After reaching the end of one line, turn the thread in the opposite direction*

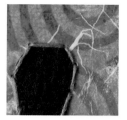
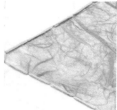

and complete an over-under pattern, creating a continuous, unbroken line. The final sewn work will look like a series of dashes.

13. Check the back of the finished piece and trim any stray threads.

Try This

When selecting papers to use in a project, remember that the more cotton in the paper, the more likely it will not bubble during the drying process. The best way to determine this is to bend and flex the papers to see how they respond under pressure. Stiffer, heavier papers are the most difficult to adhere to watercolor paper when working on a paper quilt.

Chapter 6

Dimensional Projects

The projects you will find in this chapter are a bit different because they aren't made to display on a wall. These projects take your creativity further and enable you to think outside the box. If you know someone who enjoys handmade items, why not make them a special gift or greeting? Watching his or her face light up with joy when the gift is opened is very rewarding.

In this chapter you'll find a beautiful handmade greeting card that offers a warm, personal touch and is special enough to be displayed long after the event has passed.

Do you know someone who is an avid reader? Craft a quilted paper bookmark as a gift, especially appropriate if it's tucked into a new book or journal. And speaking of journals, what better way is there to document your travels than a travel-themed journal? This project is a perfect logbook for collecting globetrotting memories. Customize one in whatever theme you desire as a thoughtful token for a special occasion.

Flowers put a smile on everyone's face—and if you can't grow them, make some instead. Paper flowers can be customized for any occasion and they last much longer. Need a great place to show off those blossoms? With a quilted vase, you have a winning combination of handmade beauty. Not only can it be used to display quilted blooms, but you could also slip a glass vase inside to showcase a real bouquet.

Quilted Greeting Card

Terri Stegmiller

5" x 6½" (12.7 x 16.5 cm)

Creating your own greeting cards is not a new concept, and there are so many materials and methods available that they've become quite simple to make. For the card in this project, you don't even have to purchase blank cardstock.

Materials

- Adhesives: permanent, temporary
- Fabric-backed paper: 10" x 6½" (25.4 x 16.5 cm)
- Inkpad: metallic
- Paper: 8½" x 11" (21.6 x 27.9 cm) assorted coordinating colors (3–4)
- Ribbon
- Thread: coordinating colors, metallic

Tools

- Bone folder
- Metal edged-ruler
- Rubber stamp: greeting
- Scissors
- Sewing machine

Instructions

Prepare the paper

1. Score and fold the fabric-backed paper in half using a bone folder and ruler.

Make the card front arrangement

2. Arrange layers of cut or torn coordinating papers on the front of the card; adhere with temporary adhesive. Stitch the background layers to the card front with a straight stitch and coordinating thread.

3. Cut or tear a heart shape from desired paper. Adhere heart to the card with temporary adhesive, and then straight stitch around the edges.

4. Cut 10–15 short lengths of metallic thread and arrange them on the heart. Adhere with permanent adhesive.

5. Cut a 12" (30.5 cm) length of ribbon. Pinch together three folds in the center of the ribbon to form three loops. Lay the ribbon on top of the metallic thread with all the loops to one side and straight stitch across the base of the loops, making sure to stitch through each fold that forms a loop. *Note: This can be done by hand or with a sewing machine.* Fluff the loops after stitching.

Make the card interior arrangement

6. Adhere paper shapes to the inside of the card where the greeting is normally located with temporary adhesive. Straight stitch shapes to secure.

7. Add more shapes as desired. Using a metallic inkpad, add glimmer around some of the edges of the shapes by applying the ink with your finger. Straight stitch these additional shapes to secure.

8. Stamp or write a greeting on a paper shape and adhere to the card with temporary adhesive. Straight stitch around the edge of the greeting to secure in place. *Note: This greeting could also be applied directly to the card.*

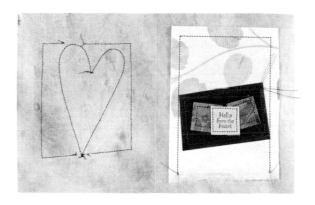

The stitching from the front of the card will show on the inside, which adds to the handcrafted feel of the project.

Try This

When you have finished with a line of stitching there will be loose threads left. Sometimes I leave the threads to add some interest and movement. Another alternative is to knot the threads on the back of the piece and trim the excess. Thread a hand-sewing needle with the thread end on the front of the project. Push the needle through to the back of the project where the other thread end is located. Tie a knot using both of the thread ends and then dab some permanent adhesive on the knot so it doesn't come undone.

The sentiment of the card can be created using different rubber stamps or simply jotting a personal note with an archival pen.

Paper Bookmark

Terri Stegmiller

2½" x 6" (6.4 x 15.2 cm)

I read a wide variety of material such as magazines and fiction, craft, and self-improvement books. There are times when I have several reading projects going on at the same time, which requires a number of bookmarks. I enjoy making bookmarks as gifts too. Whenever I present a book as a gift, I slip a bookmark inside the cover before wrapping it.

Materials

- Adhesive: temporary
- Fusible web: 2½" x 6" (6.4 x 15.2 cm) (2)
- Heavyweight interfacing: 2½" x 6" (6.4 x 15.2 cm)
- Paper: 2½" x 6" (6.4 x 15.2 cm) coordinating colors (2); assorted coordinating scraps
- Thread: black
- Yarn: 8" (20.3 cm) assorted (3–5)

Tools

- Awl
- Crochet hook
- Iron and ironing surface
- Metal-edged ruler
- Scissors
- Sewing machine

Instructions

Prepare the paper

1. Adhere the 2½" x 6" (6.4 x 15.2 cm) paper for the focal background to the interfacing with fusible web.

2. From the assorted paper scraps, cut shapes as desired.

Make the arrangement

3. Arrange the cut shapes on the background paper and adhere with temporary adhesive.

4. Using the stitch of your choice (straight, zigzag, or free motion), sew the shapes to the background.

Finish the bookmark

5. With fusible web, adhere the remaining 2½" x 6" (6.4 x 15.2 cm) paper to the backside of the interfacing.

6. Cut the corners off the top of the bookmark in an angular or curved shape, if desired.

7. Zigzag stitch around the edge of the entire bookmark.

8. Punch a hole about ½" (1.3 cm) from the top edge in the center of the top of the bookmark using the awl.

9. Lay the yarns together. Thread the crochet hook through the hole in the top of

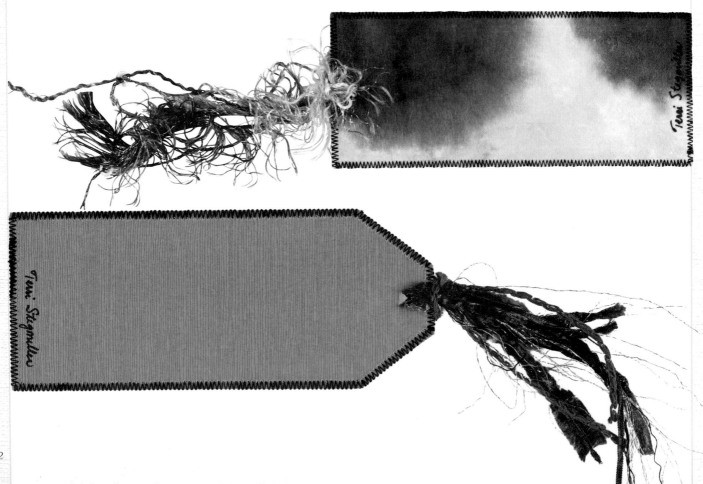

the bookmark and hook the center of the yarn length. Pull the yarns through the hole, forming a 1" (2.5 cm) loop.

10. Remove the crochet hook. Thread the fiber ends from the other side of the bookmark over the top of the bookmark and through the loop (see Fig. 1). Tighten the loop by gently tugging on the ends of the yarns. Trim yarns to desired length.

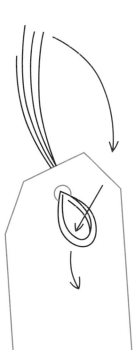

Fig. 1

Try This

For added embellishment, string a few beads onto the yarns. Personalize the bookmark with a written message or poem on the backside.

Travel Journal

Sue Bleiweiss
9¾" x 7½" (24.8 x 19.1 cm)

I like using inexpensive composition books to keep my notes because they're a comfortable size to write in and carry. The only downside is that the covers are not very attractive. This easy project gives you a lot of options for customizing your own notebook cover. Instead of using maps and letters to create a travel-themed book, consider using seed packs for a gardening journal or labels from soup or tea bag packages for a recipe journal.

Materials

- Composition book: 9¾" x 7½" (24.8 x 19.1 cm)
- Cotton fabric: coordinating color (½ yard [.46 m])
- Ephemera: book pages, letters, old maps, postcards, stamps
- Paperless fusible web: lightweight sheer
- Stabilizer: 10½" x 16½" (26.7 x 41.9 cm)
- Thread: coordinating color
- Tulle: 10½" x 16½" (26.7 x 41.9 cm) black
- Walnut ink spray
- Wool felt: 11" x 17" (27.9 x 43.2 cm) coordinating color

Tools

- Iron and ironing surface
- Metal-edged ruler
- Parchment paper
- Scissors
- Sewing machine

Instructions

Create the collage

1. Fuse a layer of fusible web to one side of the wool felt. *Note: Remember to cover your surface with parchment paper before ironing the fusible web.*

2. Tear some of the map pieces and lay them over the fused surface. Cover paper pieces with fusible web and a piece of parchment paper and iron to fuse them to the wool felt. Remove the parchment paper and repeat to add additional pieces of ephemera to the collage until you are satisfied with the design. Remove the parchment paper. *Note: If your map pages look too bright, lightly spray them with walnut ink spray and let them dry. Multiple light coats of ink are better than one heavy coat.*

3. Place the piece of tulle over the collage surface, cover with a piece of parchment paper, and fuse to the surface. Remove the parchment paper and trim the piece so it measures 10½" x 16½" (26.7 x 41.9 cm).

4. Cut a 10½" x 16½" (26.7 x 41.9 cm) piece of stabilizer and fuse it to the wrong side of the collage. Add decorative stitching or embellishments as desired but stay ½" (1.3 cm) from the edges. *Note: You'll be doing some satin stitching in this area later.*

Make the cover

5. When you have finished embellishing the cover, fuse the cotton fabric to the other side.

6. Cut two 11" x 13" (27.9 x 33 cm) pieces of fabric to make the inside pockets that hold the composition book in place. Fold each piece of fabric in half, wrong sides together, and press them to make two 11" x 6½" (27.9 x 16.5 cm) pieces. Place them on the inside along the two ends, matching the raw edges, and baste them in place using a scant ¼" (.6 cm) seam allowance.

7. Satin stitch around all the edges. *Note: I stitched around my edges twice using the widest zigzag stitch setting on my machine. Once you've finished the edges, fold the cover in half, right sides together, and slip the composition book inside.*

 Try This

When working with lightweight sheer, paperless fusible web, use a very hot iron and take your time. The more you heat the fusible web the more it will disappear from the surface and be less noticeable in the finished piece.

The green fabric used on the interior of the journal below accents the images used on the cover (shown on page 106) while the stitching around the edge literally and figuratively ties the whole project together.

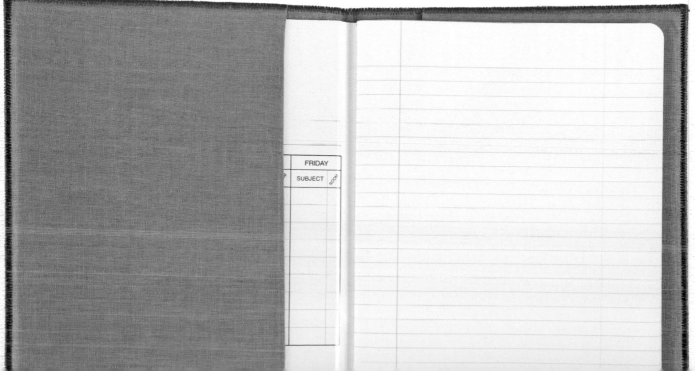

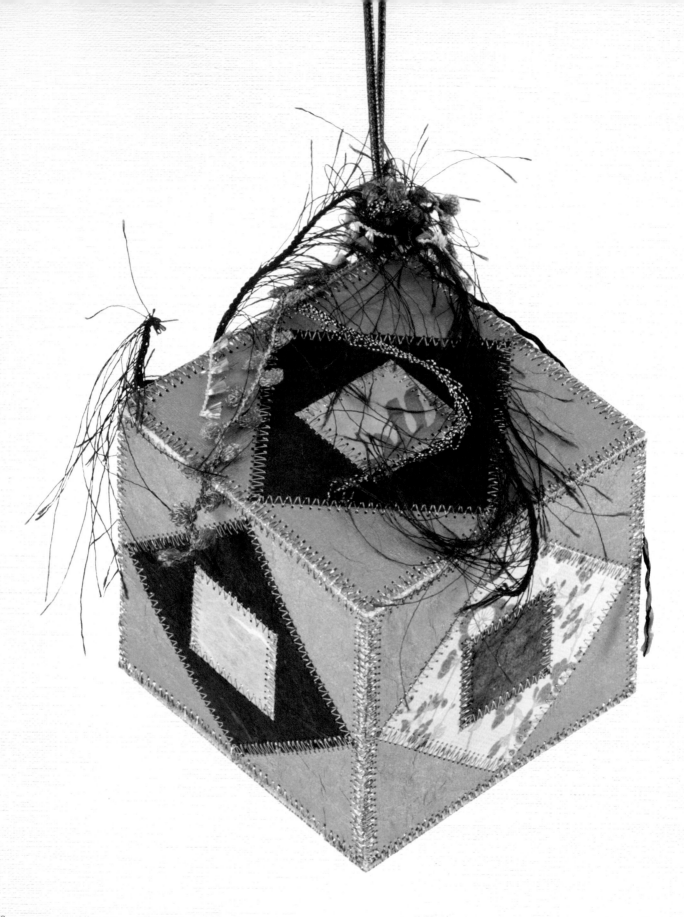

Quilt Cube Ornament

Terri Stegmiller
3" (7.6 cm) square

The holidays are such magical times and adding some handmade touches to the season makes it extra special. Handmade ornaments are one of my favorite things to make and they seem to give my holiday decor an added feeling of love, home, and family. These cubes are not only for the holidays—consider making them with a theme in mind. They'd make great wedding decorations with the addition of photocopied pictures of the bride and groom from their childhood or candid photos from their days of courtship.

Materials

- Adhesive: temporary
- Cord: coordinating color (8" [20.3 cm])
- Fusible web: 3" (7.6 cm) square (6)
- Heavyweight interfacing: 3" (7.6 cm) square (6)
- Paper: 3" (7.6 cm) square (6), assorted coordinating scraps
- Pencil
- Polyester fiberfill
- Thread: coordinating color
- Yarn: 8" (20.3 cm) assorted (5–7)

Tools

- Iron and ironing surface
- Metal-edged ruler
- Needle
- Scissors
- Sewing machine
- Thimble

Instructions

Prepare the paper

1. Adhere the 3" (7.6 cm) square papers to the heavyweight interfacing squares with fusible web, creating six panels.

2. From the assorted paper scraps, cut six 2" (5.1 cm) squares and six 1" (2.5 cm) squares.

Make the panels

3. Place a 2" (5.1 cm) square on point on one 3" (7.6 cm) square panel and adhere with temporary adhesive. Zigzag stitch around the 2" (5.1 cm) square with a coordinating thread. Repeat with the remaining five panels and 2" (5.1 cm) squares.

4. Place a 1" (2.5 cm) square on point in the center of one 2" (5.1 cm) square and adhere with temporary adhesive. Zigzag stitch around the 1" (2.5 cm) square with a coordinating thread. Repeat with the remaining five panels and 1" (2.5 cm) squares.

5. Zigzag stitch around the four sides of each 3" (7.6 cm) panel.

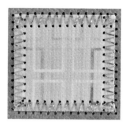

Finish the cube

6. Arrange the panels (see Fig. 1). Butt the edge of one panel against the edge of the adjacent panel. Zigzag stitch across the edges of the panels where they meet. *Note: When joining the panels together, make sure they touch but do not overlap.*

7. Join the remaining panel edges together to form the cube shape (see Fig. 2). Hand-stitch to join these edges using coordinating thread. *Note: In the following diagram the arrows point to the edges that should be joined.*

8. Before stitching the final panel, place polyester fiberfill inside to support the cube walls. *Note: Don't overstuff the ornament. You don't want the walls to bulge outward.* Hand-stitch the last panel edges together.

9. Fold the cord in half and stitch the two ends together to form a loop. Hand-stitch the loop to one corner of the cube.

10. Wrap all the yarns around the hanging cord at the base, close to the cube, to create fringe. Tie them in a simple knot and trim to desired length.

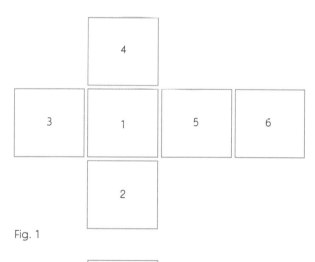

Fig. 1

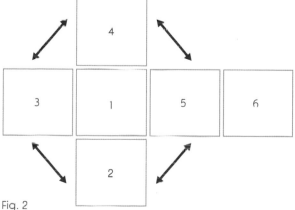

Fig. 2

Try This

When sewing panels together in Step 6, place a hand on each panel and align them next to each other. Carefully move the panels underneath the presser foot and begin sewing. As you sew down the length of the two panels, apply light pressure to the panels with your hands so they remain positioned next to each other.

Casa de Flores

Terri Stegmiller

6" x 14" (15.2 x 35.6 cm)

The title of this project is Spanish and translates to "house of flowers," which reminds me of a florist's shop. The first thing that strikes me whenever I walk into a florist's shop is the fragrance, followed by the masses of colorful flowers. This is my interpretation of a house of flowers. It will not only display paper or silk flowers; simply add a glass vase inside and you can showcase fresh flowers, too.

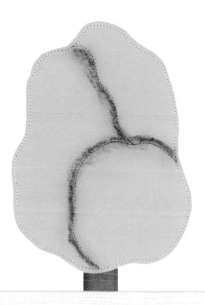

Materials

- Adhesive: temporary
- Charcoal pencil
- Fabric: 6" x 14" (15.2 x 35.6 cm) coordinating colors (4); 6" (15.2 cm) square: green
- Fabric-backed paper: 6" x 14" (15.2 x 35.6 cm) coordinating colors (4); 6" (15.2 cm) square: green
- Fusible web: 6" x 14" (15.2 x 35.6 cm) (8); 6" (15.2 cm) square (2)
- Heavyweight interfacing: 6" x 14" (15.2 x 35.6 cm) (4); 6" (15.2 cm) square
- Paper: 8½" x 11" (21.6 x 27.9 cm) assorted coordinating colors and patterns (9)
- Spray fixative
- Thread: coordinating colors (6)

Tools

- Iron and ironing surface
- Metal-edged ruler
- Needle
- Scissors
- Sewing machine
- Thimble

Instructions

Prepare the paper

1. Fuse the fabric-backed papers to the heavyweight interfacing to create the background for the four sides and bottom of the vase.

2. Cut two 4" x 9" (10.2 x 22.9 cm) rectangles from desired paper for the houses. Cut two triangles from coordinating paper for the roofs. *Note: The edge of the triangle that overlaps the house paper must be 5¼" (13.3 cm) long. The remaining two sides can be any length you desire, depending on how tall you want the roof to be.*

3. Cut eight 1½" (3.8 cm) squares of paper for the windows and two 1½" x 3" (3.8 x 7.6 cm) rectangles for the doors.

4. Cut two 1" x 6½" (2.5 x 16.5 cm) rectangles of paper for the tree trunks. Freehand cut two shapes from desired paper for the treetops.

Make the house arrangement

5. Secure the house to the background with temporary adhesive. Straight stitch along the edges of the two long sides with coordinating thread. Straight stitch horizontal lines about ½" (1.3 cm) apart from the top to the bottom on the house.

6. Adhere the roof with temporary adhesive, overlapping ¼" (.6 cm) of the top edge of the house. Straight stitch along the edges of the roof with coordinating thread.

7. Arrange the windows and door and secure them with temporary adhesive. Straight stitch along the edges of the door with a coordinating thread. Straight stitch along the edges of the windows with a coordinating thread.

8. Draw along the edges of the house, roof, windows, and door with the charcoal pencil. Smudge the lines with your finger or a paper towel to soften. Add a doorknob with the same pencil.

9. Apply a light coat of spray fixative to set the charcoal marks; let dry.

10. Repeat steps 5–9 to make a second house panel.

Make the tree arrangement

11. Secure the tree trunk to the background with temporary adhesive. Straight stitch along the edges of the two long sides with a coordinating thread.

12. Adhere the treetop to the background with temporary adhesive, overlapping ¼" (.6 cm) of the tree trunk. Straight stitch along the edges of the treetop with a coordinating thread. Add some curved lines on the interior of the tree to portray shape and depth.

13. Draw along the edges of the tree trunk and treetop with the charcoal pencil and smudge the lines.

14. Apply a light coat of spray fixative to set the charcoal marks; let dry.

15. Repeat steps 11–14 to make a second tree panel.

Finish the vase

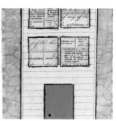

16. Fuse the fabric to the back of the interfacing.

17. Zigzag stitch around each of the four side panels and bottom piece. *Note: The recommended stitch width is 4–5 mm and the stitch length is .4–.8 mm but these may need to be adjusted, depending on the thickness of the thread used.*

18. Align one long edge of one tree panel to one long edge of a house panel and zigzag stitch from top to bottom. Flip the unit over and zigzag stitch over the same area. *Note: When joining the panels together, make sure they are touching but not overlapping.* Continue to attach panels in the same manner but alternate the designs (see Fig. 1).

19. Once all four panels are connected, hand-stitch remaining edges together, forming a square. Hand-stitch the bottom piece to the four-panel unit.

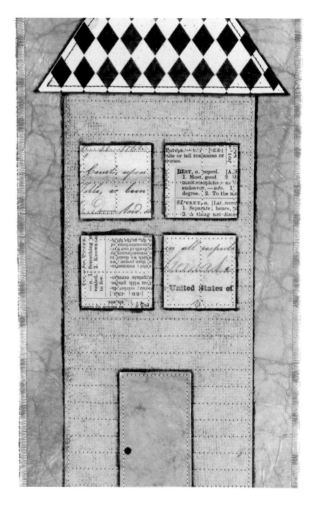

Zigzag stitch
↓

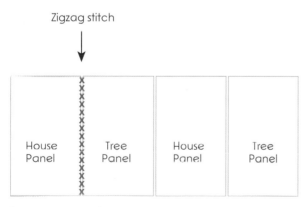

Fig. 1

✳ Try This

Personalize the vase design by drawing birds, children, flowers, pets, and other details with pens or markers.

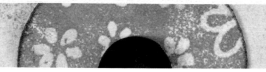

Paper Flowers

Terri Stegmiller

4½" (11.4 cm) diameter

Handmade flowers are fun to make, especially when you can make them any shape, size, and color you like. They add an air of whimsy to your decor and they don't need to be watered. Imagine the look on a friend's face when you present a gift of paper flowers. Create a bouquet of handmade flowers for table decorations at a special gathering or a seasonal bouquet to brighten a coworker's desk. Make them with shorter stems to use as tree decorations. Simply twist the stem around a branch.

Materials

- Button: ¼" shank-style coordinating color
- Floral paddle wire: 24-gauge (10" [25.4 cm])
- Floral stem wire: 20-gauge
- Floral tape: green
- Inkpads: black, metallic
- Paper: 8½" x 11" (21.6 x 27.9 cm) assorted coordinating colors and patterns (6)
- Paperless fusible web: 8½" x 11" (21.6 x 27.9 cm) (3)
- Thread: coordinating color

Tools

- Awl
- Iron and ironing surface
- Metal-edged ruler
- Pencil
- Scissors
- Sewing machine
- Template plastic
- Wire cutters

Instructions

Prepare the paper

1. Sandwich a sheet of paperless fusible web between the wrong sides of two coordinating papers and lay on the ironing surface. Press firmly with the iron to bond the sheets together. Repeat this step to create three double-sided sheets of paper.

2. Draw a 4½" circle, 2¾" circle, and 1⅜" circle onto the template plastic and cut them out. Trace the templates onto the double-sided papers and cut them out. *Note: You need three circles per flower, one from each template size.*

Create the flower head

3. Distress the edges of the paper circles by rubbing the paper's edges on the inkpads until you have the desired color; let dry. *Note: Alternate between the inkpads for each size of circle.*

4. Cut petal shapes around the edges of one or more of the three circles. Cut V shapes straight in from the edges or gentle curves for a softer look. *Note: Be careful not to cut too far into the center of the circle.*

5. Sew around the edges of one or more of the three circles using either a straight or zigzag stitch.

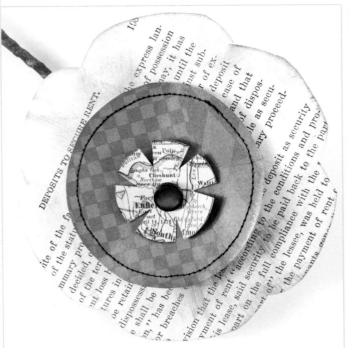

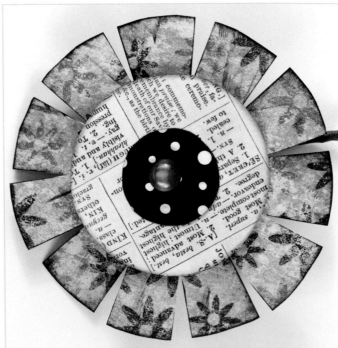

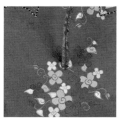

Assemble the flower

6. Center and lay the three circles on top of each other with the largest on the bottom and the smallest on the top. Punch a hole in the center of all three circles using the awl.

7. String the button onto a 10" (25.4 cm) length of floral paddle wire. Center the button on the wire and fold the wires in half. Twist the wire two to three times underneath the button to secure it. Push the wire ends through the holes in the paper circles and slide them up so the button sits snugly against the paper. Hold the wire just below the flower to keep the paper petals and button in place for the next step.

8. Position the paper flower at the end of a floral stem wire and start twisting the paddle wire around the stem to secure the flower to the stem. Keep twisting until the entire stem is covered; cut the wire.

9. Attach the floral tape to the stem about ¼" (.6 cm) under the flower, wrapping it around the stem in an upward motion toward the flower. Wrap tape five to seven times around the stem as close to the flower as possible to help support it, then slowly start wrapping in a downward direction and continue to wrap until all of the paddle wire is covered. Tear the floral tape and wrap the tape end onto the stem.

Let your creativity and imagination extend to the back of the flower. Choose a contrasting background to add a little zing to the arrangement or use one paper for all the flower backs for a more uniform display.

 Try This

Add some folds and bends to the flower petals after the project is assembled to create movement and dimension. Bend the floral stem wire just below the flower head to point the blossom a specific direction.

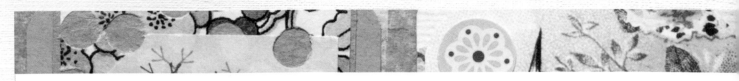

Templates

Vellum Vase Patterns

Enlarge Vase 110%
Flower Actual Size

Garden Breeze Patterns

Actual Size

Patty Patterns
Enlarge 130%

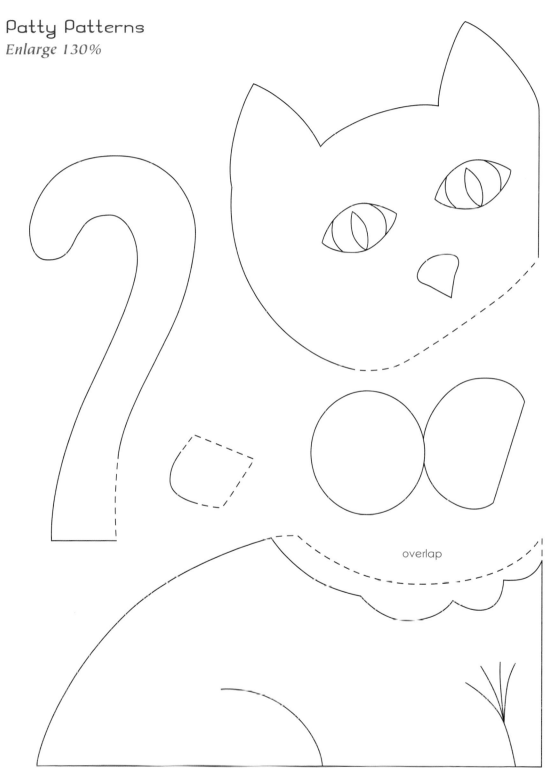

overlap

Boris Patterns
Enlarge 110%

Women's Wishing Quilt Patterns
Actual Size

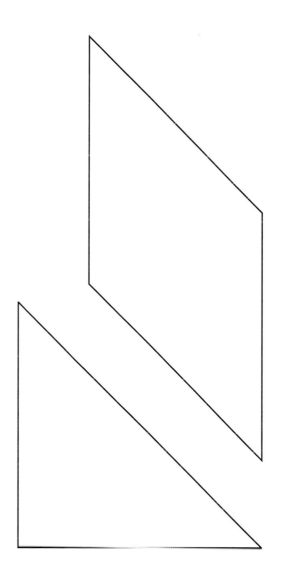

Art Figure Pattern
Actual Size

About the Author

Because of her mother, grandmothers, and aunt, Terri Stegmiller has been surrounded by creativity her entire life. She didn't always enjoy sewing and those segments in her school home economic classes were definitely not her favorite. Some of her early crafting interests included counted cross-stitch and crochet.

Terri first became interested in quilting around 1994. Her mother-in-law always seemed to have a quilting project in the making and Terri would watch and ask questions. The first bed quilt Terri made turned out to be quite the learning experience. Tackling the project on her own and not knowing any better, she used two fluffy layers of quilt batting to achieve the puff quilt look known as trapunto. The quilt took a few years to finish, but she did get it done and has learned a lot since. After deciding that she didn't have the patience to make bed-sized quilts, she turned to wall-sized quilts. Terri's home is filled with her own quilted wall hangings.

Terri has become interested in several types of crafts, such as cloth doll making, polymer clay, beading, decorating gourds, mosaic, and more. She has recently re-discovered knitting and has a growing interest in drawing, painting, and mixed media arts. Terri is mostly self-taught and has taken a few online and local classes. She loves learning new techniques and is always willing to go shopping for supplies.

Terri is the assistant publisher of *Fibre & Stitch*, an online mixed-media magazine. Her work has appeared in *Soft Dolls & Animals, Haute Handbags 2*, and *1,000 Artist Trading Cards: Innovative and Inspired Mixed Media ATCs*. She also does some teaching, both online and locally.

To see more of Terri's work, visit www.terristegmiller.com or http://stegart.blogspot.com.

Terri lives in Mandan, North Dakota, with her husband, son, and five cats on ten acres, where she enjoys flower gardening and bird watching.

Contributors

Sue Bleiweiss — *Page 104*

Fiber artist Sue Bleiweiss enjoys spending her days in the studio experimenting with different surface design techniques and materials to create unique fabrics and surfaces to use in her artwork. She loves to create three-dimensional pieces such as boxes, vases, sketchbooks, and journals. Every journal and sketchbook she creates is unique and designed to be personal and special to the user.

One of Sue's greatest pleasures is passing along what she's learned and developed by teaching online classes in fiber arts and surface design as well as publishing an online mixed-media fiber arts magazine called *Fibre & Stitch*. She has had several projects published in national magazines including Interweave Press' *Quilting Arts* and *Handwoven* as well as several *Stampington* publications. Several of her pieces reside in private collections throughout the world.

Sue lives in Upton, Massachusetts, with her very supportive husband and lots of dogs. Visit her website at www.suebleiweiss.com.

Zana Clark — *Pages 68, 78, and 86*

Zana Clark is an award-winning multimedia artist specializing in a line of unique original art stamp designs. She has displayed her myriad creations in numerous galleries and gift stores in the Midwest and has participated in hundreds of juried art fairs and rubber stamp conventions around the country.

Throughout her artistic phases, Zana has combined stamped images with a variety of art mediums. She decided to turn her Art Nouveau and Art Deco design-oriented imagery into an original line of elegant art rubber stamps. In June 1996, after 22 years as an art educator and school administrator, she set up her rubber art stamp company, Stamp Zia.

Zana has been featured on HGTV's Decorating with Style and has been published in numerous stamping magazines including *Rubberstampmadness*, *The Rubber Stamper*, *Stamping Arts and Crafts*, and *Vamp Stamp News*. Authors Sharilyn Miller, Suzanne McNeil, and Suze Weinberg have featured her stamp images and teaching techniques in some of their books. Zana also teaches her unique art workshops across the United States and Canada.

Zana lives in Franklin, Wisconsin.

Cathy Collier — *Page 60*

Cathy Collier began creating paper quilts after being inspired by the emerging craft community of women on the Internet. She has always loved the feel of textured paper. She started out creating small, collaged pieces and turned them into gift cards for birthdays and holidays. Cathy soon realized she could connect the tiny collaged gift cards together in the same way that a quilter might assemble a quilt.

Cathy's favorite part of each quilt is the search for and discovery of colorful vintage papers for each project. It is the most challenging part of creating a piece, but the hunt is her biggest motivation. In its beginning stages, each paper quilt is like an unsolved mystery. Each step draws her closer to the completion of a piece and unravels the mystery just a bit more.

Cathy is involved in organizing and participating in a biannual fine art show featuring the work of fifteen amazing women from different walks of life. She shows her work in various places throughout her community each year. Her online art shop, www.phantomcrimes.etsy.com, also keeps her busy.

Cathy lives in Chattanooga, Tennessee.

Colleen Kong-Savage
Pages 40, 46, and 52

Colleen Kong-Savage was born in 1973 in Hawaii and grew up in various parts of the world including Zambia, Japan, Taiwan, and Malaysia. She earned a Bachelor of Arts degree at Smith College, then an MFA in fiction writing at Columbia University. Her work has been shown in various New York establishments, including the Edward Hopper House, Joyce SoHo, and the National Arts Club. Colleen has designed several murals for public elementary schools. Currently, she is writing and illustrating her first children's story.

Colleen likes the quilt form because it's tied to tradition and has a sense of connection that comes from being passed from generation to generation. She likes paper for its simultaneous fragility and strength. In her experience, quilting is a form of collaged self-portraiture, a metaphor for many experiences pulled into a single, multi-faceted identity. As an artist exploring the idea of community, she focuses on quilts because of their connotation of individuals coming together such as quilting bees or the national AIDS quilt.

Colleen lives in Manhattan, New York, with her husband and son and works as a visual artist involved in painting, drawing, printmaking, and creating multimedia works.

Carol White
Pages 74, 82, and 90

A Chicago, Illinois, native and graduate of Herron School of Art in Indianapolis, Carol White has completed advanced degrees in fine arts and art education and has worked extensively with museums, schools, and other cultural organizations for more than twenty years.

When Carol saw the textiles created by the Quilters of Gee's Bend, Alabama, she became inspired to explore something new using mixed media. After meeting the quilters, Carol was transported back in time as memories of her great-grandmother flashed through her mind. As a tribute to her, and inspired by the Quilters of Gee's Bend, Carol started designing paper quilts.

Carol has received multiple awards for her work as an artist and educator. Among her accomplishments is the design and completion of two public art projects in Indianapolis and a Christmas tree ornament for the White House in Washington, DC.

Carol resides in Indianapolis, Indiana, and works as the assistant director of Art Education Programs. For more information, visit www.artbycarolwhite.com.

Index

Notes on Suppliers

Usually, the supplies you need for making the projects in Lark books can be found at your local craft supply store, discount mart, home improvement center, or retail shop relevant to the topic of the book. Occasionally, however, you may need to buy materials or tools from specialty suppliers. In order to provide you with the most up-to-date information, we have created a list of suppliers on our website, which we update on a regular basis. Visit us at www.larkbooks.com, click on "Craft Supply Sources," and then click on the relevant topic. You will find numerous companies listed with their web address and/or mailing address and phone number.